WALLS ARE FOR LEAPING

Dorothy Pape

An OMF Book

First printed.......... 1983

ISBN 0 85363 150 6

OMF BOOKS are distributed by
OMF, 404 South Church Street,
Robesonia, Pa 19551, USA
and
OMF, Belmont, The Vine,
Sevenoaks, Kent, TN13 3TZ, UK
and other OMF offices.

Published by Overseas Missionary Fellowship, Belmont, The Vine, Sevenoaks, Kent,
TN13 3TZ, UK
Typeset and produced by Eastern Universities Press Sdn. Bhd., Singapore
Printed by Richard Clay (S.E. Asia) Pte Ltd, Singapore

Acknowledgments

My very grateful thanks are due to Anton and Bernice Netland for all the information and verification provided for this story, and to Lorna Edwards and the Steve Metcalfs for their helpfulness in arranging my personal interviews with the Tamuras, and the other missionaries of both TEAM and OMF who supplied additional information. Many thanks too to Greg and Marcia Clapp for hospitality and help in research during much of the writing of this book, and to Mary Weston for proof-reading it.

Contents

Introduction

Would that phone call never come?

I tried, as unobtrusively as possible, to shift my weight from one numb hip and cramped knee to the other as we sat on the straw-matted floor of the Japanese living-room. How would I ever be able to take notes in this agonizing, semi-kneeling position, I began to wonder.

From years of practice my companions sat apparently comfortably in the polite ceremonial position, chatting happily with our hosts, Shooji Tamura and his wife. At last the phone rang, and Shooji hurried out to answer it.

'Michiko's very sorry for the delay,' he said as he came back. 'She's had an urgent problem to deal with at the Colony. A deaf-mute girl was sent there recently, and she often cries, and packs her bags and tries to leave. It's always been in the daytime before, and they could easily find her and bring her back. But now she has disappeared in the dark, and Michiko and two other Colony cars have been out looking for her. But she asks you to go over there now, anyway.'

It was just a short distance to the Aomori Colony for the Handicapped, and we drove past various buildings in the darkness until Shooji finally stopped outside a house on the opposite side of the street from the main entrance to the Colony.

The outer door stood open, and Shooji stepped inside and slid open the inner door a little, calling through it the customary 'Gomen-kudasai' to announce our arrival. Then came the invitation to enter, and I failed miserably in the attempt to step gracefully out of my own closely-fitting shoes up the nine-inch-high step into the heel-less guest slippers placed ready outside the inner door. Shooji ushered us in, and then introduced us to his brother-in-law, Michiko's husband of just over a year, whom my friends had not yet met. Then we learned that Michiko herself had been called away again to the Colony office in connection with the missing deaf-mute girl.

After the introductory bows we were motioned across the room to a door at the left of the rear wall, and Shooji bid us goodbye. Here again we had to take a big step up, leaving our slippers below, and found ourselves in a cosy *tatami*-floored room (the traditional thick straw mat). With secret joy I saw on one side of the room a heavy wooden cabinet with a firm door against which I could lean to write notes.

Finally settled, I eyed Michiko's husband with special interest as he courteously served tea and cookies. Of slight build, he yet gave the impression of muscular strength, and had a pleasant smile. Glasses and a small thinning spot on the back of his head suggested a man in his early forties. He had been born in southern Japan, I knew, and it seemed an unusual succession of events must have brought him so far north, only a year ago, as Michiko Tamura's husband.

My thoughts were interrupted by the rattle of the outer door as it slid open on its steel runners. Was it Michiko at last?

Her husband pushed back the paper door of the room we were in, and there was Michiko, full of apology for her absence on our arrival. Her face arrested attention at once. She had the large, round type most common among Japanese women, but it was her eyes which gave her such an attractive appearance. They were still sparkling, even after a long day of worrisome problems, and there was a kind, cheerful quality about them. Her mouth was small and firm. Her smile revealed the familiar Japanese shiny gold caps and fillings in a few of her teeth, but she hardly looked her 42 years.

She was dressed in a kind of purple sleeveless jerkin or vest of interesting design, worn over a white crepe blouse which covered unusually powerful-looking shoulders; beneath were well-cut slacks of a grey mixture.

As she finished apologizing, she leaned her crutches against the corner formed by the wall and the steep steps, put her hands on the *tatami* and dexterously hitched herself up into the room. Her legs came trailing behind, as floppy and useless as those of a stuffed rag doll.

I had to be formally introduced, of course, and once more we went through the deep, forehead-to-floor bow, repeated three times. Then it transpired that I was not on the correct side of the room for the honored guest! I hastily pleaded age and infirmity for my chosen position in front of the cupboard, and being well used to foreigners and their uncouth ways Michiko graciously accepted the explanation without demur.

As we drank tea Michiko explained that although the deaf-mute girl hadn't yet been found, she had just finished telephoning all the city taxi companies, asking them to alert all drivers not to take any girl of that description to the railway station, but return her to the Colony. So between that and the two Colony cars still out, she was sure the girl would soon be found.

We asked her if her evenings were often disturbed like this, and she smiled. 'Quite often. I frequently don't get time for myself until 11 p.m.'

She then explained that she was not only one of the founders and directors of the Colony but had sixteen handicapped women, including this deaf one aged 23, directly under her care, both as her students in the sewing school department and for personal counselling for their many problems. Again the smile came as she added that in her own earlier life the great problem had been merely to stay alive. Those in the Colony now were provided food, shelter and training, so only had 'luxury problems' — how they could get a husband, become independent or change an uncongenial room-mate.

We were just nicely into the intriguing story of Michiko's early life in a pioneering family on Japan's northernmost island of Karafuto, opposite the coast of Siberia, when the phone rang in the outer room.

Michiko had been opposite me across the quilt-covered heater, sitting firm and upright in the usual Japanese position, those useless legs tucked out of sight beneath her. Now, as she swung herself rapidly along the straw matting by her strong arms and hands, I thought that Japanese-style housing was perhaps wonderfully suited for people handicapped in this way. Later I was to realize that the constant changing of footwear from stocking feet to slippers to outdoor shoes, and the impossibility of using a wheel chair because of the various floor levels and the treasured straw matting, made it a very real hardship.

Worst of all, however, was the normal Japanese attitude to handicapped people, for until quite recently they were regarded as 'damaged goods' and therefore worthless and unwanted, little better than animals. Somehow a physical handicap often seems to suggest to others that the person must be mentally subnormal too. The fate of such persons had therefore usually been to be completely shut away at home, out of sight of the general public.

Back in 1890 the famous Russian doctor and author, Anton Chekhov, had paid a three-month visit to Michiko's native island, which had recently become a Russian possession known to them as Sakhalin. Apart from being the site of three of their notorious penal colonies, it was largely uninhabited except for a few tribal people. After a most difficult journey across forests, mountains and marshland, Chekhov finally reached the east coast, and not far from the spot which forty years later was to be Michiko's birthplace he wrote:

> 'This is the Pacific Ocean. On this bank of the Naybuchi river there can be heard the sound of convicts hacking·away with their axes..... and far away there lies the coast of America. To the left through the fog you can see the headlands of Sakhalin, to the right more cliffs, ... and not a single soul around you..... You ask yourself for whom do these waves roar, what are they calling for, and for whom will they roar when you have gone away.....'*

As the Pacific breakers thunder against the craggy coastal cliffs of her native Karafuto, so it seemed the waves of adversity had roared and beaten upon the life of Michiko Tamura. She told me she had often thought she must have been 'hewn out of rock' by God, to be able to survive so many blows and obstacles. 'Rocklike' she certainly seems in one sense, or even obstinate and headstrong as her family so often thought her in the early days. Yet her strong will has most often been directed towards herself in setting high, sometimes seemingly impossible goals. After becoming a Christian she believed that most of her goals were God-given and motivated by a desire to serve Him. So when family, friends and church leaders all tried to discourage her she would just whisper, 'Well it's Your responsibility, Lord, if I fail.' In time she came to share the secret of the Psalmist's triumph in adversity: 'By my God I have leaped over a wall.'

Her telephone conversation finished, Michiko joined us again under the wadded quilt, telling us the missing girl had been found and was being driven home. We had time for only a few more details of her early life when we heard the rattle of the outer door being pushed open, and a voice calling *'Sensei!'* A kind-faced assistant warden had come in, holding the arm of the deaf-mute girl who stood choking with sobs, her straggly hair pulled down over her eyes so that it was quite impossible to see her face.

*Anton Chekhov, *The Island: A journey to Sakhalin*

How does one communicate anything to a person suffering perhaps the most frustrating handicap known to man, without the aid of sign language or lip-reading ability? How would Michiko handle the situation, we wondered. Then we saw. On the hard linoleum in the cold by the still-partly-open front door, Michiko went straight down on her knees, her forehead bowed to the floor in front of this poor sobbing young woman.

What would this gesture mean to her? It could be saying that this one who had caused them all so much trouble and anxiety was welcomed back as an honored member by the *Sensei* (teacher and leader); or even perhaps that she was being offered a sincere apology that they hadn't been able to make her happy in their midst, and would make greater efforts in future.

Having already arranged a time to meet next day, we hastily murmured goodnight and slipped out into the darkness, praying in our hearts for God's guidance for Michiko in this particular problem.

Once in the car, however, there was a general feeling of excitement, for the early details of Michiko's life had whetted our interest for what was to follow. There was undoubted evidence of unusual personal courage and initiative, plus fortitude displayed by the whole family in the face of great adversity. There were intriguing hints of pioneer life in one of the most remote islands of the world on which few Westerners other than Russians have ever set foot; while the time span included one of the most cataclysmic periods in international history. Above all there were the heart-warming signs of God at work in a wonderful way. Intuitively we all felt that here indeed would be a story worth telling.

THE TAMURA FAMILY

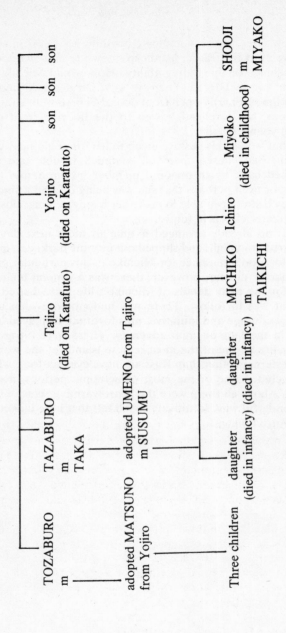

Chapter One

Calamity Strikes

UMENO TAMURA HASTILY LOCKED THE DOOR of the large grocery store after her departing assistants. It was a warm August evening in 1936, but Mototomari village lay on the east coast of the island of Sakhalin (or Karafuto as its southern half was called by its Japanese settlers), and she turned towards the sea hoping to feel a refreshing breeze. After a hot, busy day inside she ached with tiredness; in fact, she felt she had never recovered her full strength since the birth of her son Ichiro, months ago now. She took some deep breaths of the faint breeze from the Pacific Ocean which lapped against the shore a few yards away, then hurried anxiously towards the family quarters behind the store.

She found her mother, Taka, alone in the living-room except for little Ichiro crawling at her feet. The others had already eaten, and as Taka brought in Umeno's supper she seemed unusually silent and preoccupied. The question burning in her daughter's mind remained unasked, and soon the older woman disappeared into her bedroom at the back of the house. She returned in a few minutes.

'Miko-chan* still doesn't seem well — in fact she's really feverish,' she said, her face puckered with anxiety.

Umeno felt her heart miss a beat at this news of her daughter.

'It's probably just a chill,' she managed to say with studied calm. 'The weather has been so changeable lately, and all this rain and unaccustomed heat can't do anyone any good.'

She certainly hoped that was all it was, but Taka's expression strengthened her own uneasiness. She poured herself another cup of

*Chan — a term of endearment for a small child.

green tea, thankful she could sit undisturbed a few minutes longer. Her husband Susumu was on a 24-hour shift on the railway, and her father, Tazaburo Tamura, was at a business meeting at the local temple.

It was a relief to let her thoughts wander a little after the demands and distractions of the store, and she quickly drew Ichiro to her and gave him a surreptitious hug after her mother had left the room again What a comfort it was to have him, and Michiko, but she still sorrowed secretly for the two baby girls now in the temple burying ground. Each had been born healthy, but somehow she had been unable to nurse them properly, and in those early pioneering days no other milk was available. There was little livestock industry, because in that mainly Buddhist culture eating flesh was considered 'an evil and disgusting habit'. So she had had to watch, broken-hearted, as each baby had gradually weakened from lack of nourishment.

At last Michiko had been born and had survived, a healthy cute little girl full of energy and mischief, and an early talker who quickly made friends with everyone she met. It was hard to imagine her sick now, and Umeno longed to go and see her.

'Is there anything I can do for her?' she asked hesitantly as her mother just then appeared again.

'No,' came the sharp reply. 'It's best she should be kept quiet, so she can sleep as much as possible.'

Umeno's mother-heart ached, but she knew it was useless to protest. In those days in Japan children were still regarded as belonging to the extended family, in particular the grandparents, rather than to their own mothers and fathers, and the Tamura family was a perfect example of this practice.

In days of rapid change in the last third of the 19th century,* an enterprising couple named Tamura had obtained a good piece of property in a small fishing village called Kominato, about an hour's journey around the coast from the provincial capital of Aomori in the north of Japan's main island of Honshu. This city was the important terminal of the new railway connecting the north-east of the country with Tokyo, as well as being the port for access to the island of Hokkaido. The Tamuras also acquired land in the foothills a couple of miles outside their village, and painstakingly developed it into terraced rice fields. Unlike land further south, Aomori fields could only produce one harvest a year because of the long severe winters, but the government was encouraging the development of all possible arable

---

*See Appendix I

land to meet the needs of the rapidly increasing population.

The Tamuras worked hard, and were further blessed with seven sons who became a great help in developing the land, until each in turn had to serve his time in military service. As they returned from this, however, marriages had to be arranged for them and it was soon obvious that the fields would not sustain all these potential new families. The eldest son's family would stay with the parents, of course, and work the farm, but what about the rest? Serious discussion soon began in the family councils as to what plans should be made for the future.

Those were heady and exciting days for the Japanese people. Emperor Meiji had proved a wise and liberal ruler, and Japan was well on the way to becoming a world power. Her adaptability and industry gained her the title of 'The miracle people of the age, the hope of Asia, the British of the East.' Her mercantile marine sailed every ocean and fishing, textile, electrical and petroleum industries were well established. The first general elections had been held, and compulsory education was being introduced.

Abroad, Japanese influence was beginning to be felt in Korea and Manchuria, and their army was the major force rescuing the foreigners caught in the Boxer uprising in China in 1900, thus making their nation even more admired in the west. Further victories forced the Chinese to cede Formosa to them and finally, to the astonishment of the world, in 1904 the Japanese attacked and decisively beat the Russian navy. In the terms of the Treaty of Portsmouth which ended this conflict, South Sakhalin was ceded to Japan by the Russians. Five years later, Japan annexed Korea too.

Now colonizers were urgently needed to secure these new Japanese possessions and develop them economically. They would also provide a means of livelihood for the population which was suddenly increasing, after centuries of stagnation or even decrease, due to various epidemics and famines in the long Tokugawa era.

The Tamura family considered the matter carefully from every angle. Should one or more of the sons take advantage of the government's persuasive offer to go to the new colony of Karafuto, or South Sakhalin?

'It's cold, wet and foggy,' objected Tazaburo's mother. 'Why, even Japanese traders used to refuse to spend the winter there!'

'Yes, that's true,' her son agreed. 'But after all, we're used to the cold. We were all born here in snowy Aomori prefecture.'

'And it sounds a good place to live in other ways,' joined Tajiro the third son. 'They say there are rich coal deposits, huge quantities of fish, virgin forests and sheltered valleys suitable for agriculture. And some of our neighbors are planning to go too, so we won't be alone.'

'What if anything happens to Tozaburo?' his mother asked.

'Tazaburo would have to come home and take his place.'

'Well, it's only 25 miles across the strait from Hokkaido,' Tazaburo told her. 'It's much nearer than Formosa or Korea, where other settlers are going, and I could come back easily if I had to.'

So finally it was settled that Tazaburo, Tajiro and Yojiro would go to Karafuto. There was one further matter to be settled, however. Neither of the two older sons yet had any children, while the third and fourth sons, though married later, already had two each. So it was decided that Yojiro should give one of his daughters to Tozaburo, and Tajiro should give his daughter Umeno to Tazaburo and his wife, Taka. This was a common practice in Japan then. What the feelings of the natural mother may sometimes have been, we can only guess; but the foundation of the social order in Japan was, as Lafcadio Herzan once expressed it: 'The household rules the person; the five-family group the household; the community the group.'

Before they left, Tazaburo's family were able also to obtain for him the promise of an orphan boy named Susumu who would stay with relatives also in Karafuto, and later be adopted into the family to marry the adopted Umeno. Thus, barring some fatality, the family name would be assured of continuance in the new country, and the ancestors would be guaranteed someone to care for them well into the future.

So in 1914 this newly-formed family set out for Karafuto. In the previous decade it was mainly farmers who had been encouraged to go there. From 1914 onwards, however, the emphasis was more on forestry and fishing for the teeming harvests of herring, trout, salmon, cod, scallops and king crab.

Perhaps because of the location of his old home, Tazaburo Tamura chose to settle on the east coast, in a little fishing village called Mototomari. Unlike much of the eastern coastline with its high rugged cliffs which had so impressed Chekhov, here there was a little bay which provided shelter and comparatively calm water for fishing boats. There was also enough flat land for village homes to be built, and eventually a railway track, before the ground rose in a steep cliff west of them. Up there the settlers had begun to clear the land of the scrawny, gale-swept larch and fir, in order to plant fields and vegetable gardens. But beyond these, the trees soon became thick forest on the foothills of the long mountain range which bisected the island from north to south.

Tazaburo quickly realized that he had no wish to be a fisherman, and it gradually came to light that his hard early start developing the family fields at home, and then his military service, had weakened him physically so that he was now not equal to the hard pioneering work required to establish a farm. In addition, all settlers were expected to contribute labor for the construction of schools, parks, clinics, shrines and temples in the larger communities.

Fortunately a new railway was being pushed northwards from the capital city Toyohara in the south, along the coast through Mototomari towards the border with Russian Sakhalin. So Tazaburo was able to get less strenuous work as a railway official. Even so he suffered a bad heart attack at 44 and had to retire. As more and more people came to settle there, however, the enterprising Tamuras realized the potential of a grocery store. Taka also had the recipe of a special kind of cake very popular with the Japanese so, what with baking these and the increasing sale of groceries, the family eventually became quite comfortably off. The east and south coasts were ice-bound eight months of the year, so supplies from the mainland could only come in the four summer months. Good business foresight, or inspired guesswork, was required to estimate the needs of the burgeoning population for the following year and soon the Tamuras had to add storerooms to accommodate their large summer supplies.

When he was old enough the adopted boy Susumu also joined the railway as an engineer, and was married to Umeno. With the absence of any roads through the island's dense forests, swamps and mountains, more and more railway tracks were laid and soon Mototomari became quite an important depot with double lines north and south.

In 1928 the Governor of Karafuto had again made strenuous efforts to attract new farmers. Each arriving family was allowed up to 25 acres of land, with full ownership to be granted after five years provided sixty percent was then under cultivation. Free tools were available, and technical advice from newly-built agricultural research stations. Barley, buckwheat, beans and potatoes were grown, and even a little dairy farming attempted, but Karafuto was never able to become self-sufficient in food.

Taka Tamura was a strong and determined person and even when the family was successfully launched in business she continued to work a large vegetable garden up on the cliff. This provided winter supplies of carrots, potatoes and *daikon* (huge white radish weighing several pounds) which in various pickled forms constitute a main item of Japanese diet. In addition there might be beans, cabbage, cucumbers and beet in summer.

So, on the whole, life had become much less difficult. True, the climate was hard with long icy winters, then frequent rain, and mosquitoes and flies in summer. But the Tamuras were doing well financially, had a large warm house and an increasingly varied diet, while with the store to run they were not bored in the long winters. In addition there was the satisfaction of seeing their adopted country increasingly prosperous. In fact, in this very year of 1936 for the first time Karafuto was no longer subsidized by the government in Tokyo.

Above all, after the bitter sorrow of the death of two babies, Michiko had been born and a new generation was launched in the Tamura family. Taka, never having known the joy of bearing a child herself, at once assumed possession of Michiko, leaving Umeno to carry on the main responsibility in the store. In imagination, Taka could already see a future husband brought into the family to marry Michiko and continue the ancestor worship.

Then an even greater cause for joy had been the birth of a son, Ichiro, who had survived because Umeno had taken good care that the wonderful foreign canned milk for babies should be included in their stock from the mainland. All in all, the future was looking bright indeed, and there was nothing to warn of the successive waves of adversity which would soon strike their family, their community and the whole country.

Michiko, three and a half years old now, had complained of feeling sick two days ago, which was not unusual for a small child. But today she was apparently still no better. As Umeno finished clearing and washing the dishes she fervently hoped it was nothing serious, and that it would not affect Ichiro. She saw he was looking sleepy now, and since she herself felt so tired and there seemed no hope of seeing Michiko, she decided to go to bed too. Her husband would not be home until early morning and her mother hadn't appeared again, so after uttering a quick prayer to the image of Amida in the small shrine on the shelf in the living room, Umeno picked up Ichiro and went into their bedroom. There she pulled two thick cotton-filled mattresses from the wall cupboard and spread them on the mat-covered floor, then placed the folded, lighter quilts in readiness on top. It was still very warm but she knew it might suddenly cool off in the night.

Next morning, as Umeno carefully stepped around her sleeping husband and quietly slid open the door into the hall she saw her mother beckoning in an agitated way.

'Miko-chan can't walk,' she whispered. 'She says her legs won't move!'

'Can't walk?' Umeno repeated anxiously. She couldn't remember ever hearing of such a thing happening to other children in the village. 'Perhaps she's just weak from the fever. Why not take her to the clinic though?' she added.

Her mother frowned. 'We'll wait another day, and see if the fever goes.'

But next day Michiko was no better. Never before had she been content to lie still for so long, and when some of her little friends came and called her name from outside she took no notice. Her grandmother, in great agitation now, put a warm kimono around her and carried her on her back to the clinic. The nurse there was mystified too, but expressed concern.

'You should take her to the hospital for diagnosis. Don't waste any time,' she urged. 'There's a good one up at Shiritori.'

Taka hurried home to discuss the matter with her husband and Umeno, and finally it was decided she should take the early afternoon train up north. Tazaburo's younger brother, Tajiro, was working for a big paper mill company there and if necessary she could spend the night with his family. So, hastily packing a few things in a cloth square, Taka tied Michiko on her back again and set off for the station, which was just a few yards from their back entrance. Michiko managed to take a bit of interest in this new adventure, but while her little arms clung round her grandmother's neck, her legs just hung, ominously helpless.

Shiritori, the nearest large town to Mototomari, was about fifty miles further north. There the cliffs were even further from the shoreline, leaving enough flat land for easy building and expansion into a small city, with the development of a large paper mill employing many men.

Taka had quite a long wait at the hospital but was promised she could have Michiko examined that day. At last they were called into the doctor's office.

He carefully took down all the answers to his questions, then shook his head slightly, as if puzzled. Swivelling around in his chair he reached for a large medical volume and scanned its pages for a few minutes.

'Ah — this is it!' he exclaimed at last. 'Poliomyelitis, or infantile paralysis.' He paused, then closed the book and looked up at Taka.

'There is no known cure for it,' he added with a note of finality.

Chapter Two

The Search for a Cure

TAKA TAMURA TIED MICHIKO on her back again and with an expressionless face walked out of the hospital. Emotions such as joy, sorrow, vexation and pain were not things for public exposure and a Japanese smile may often hide deep chagrin or a breaking heart. Inside, however, Taka's mind was a whirling tangle of mixed emotions. She had been so joyful about Michiko's birth and had been like a mother to her. In fact it wasn't until Michiko went to school that she became aware she was the child of her own parents and not of her grandparents. Her mother had always seemed to be busy in the store, while her father was rarely at home and always appeared cool towards her. But probably this was largely due to the possessive attitude of the grandparents; Michiko actually slept in their room until her grandfather's death, when she was nearly twenty years old.

But now, after Taka had experienced so much joy, this cruel blow had fallen. 'Now it will be impossible to arrange a marriage for Michiko,' she thought — for the usual Japanese opinion of handicapped persons is that they are 'damaged goods', little more than animals. 'Why, oh why were my husband and I not able to have children of our own, instead of having to depend on adopted ones who seem incapable of producing healthy offspring?'

Then she remembered how cute and lively Michiko had been up until now and her heart smote her as she wondered whether the child had understood the full import of the doctor's words. She looked over her shoulder to try to glimpse the face of the little girl on her back, and was relieved to see she had already fallen asleep with the motion of her grandmother's walk. There just *must* be a way to make those limp, unresponsive legs, which she could feel dangling and bobbing against her back, alive and strong again.

Taka Tamura was a resourceful woman, and she wasn't altogether sure that one could trust this new-fangled western medicine with its long, strange-sounding names. There would be no train back tonight now so they must stay with Tajiro's family; but there was certainly one thing she could do first which might be a help. That was to visit the big temple of the Jodo Shin Buddhist sect to which her family belonged.

As she approached it, she stopped to pick up the long-handled dipper from the water container and automatically rinsed her hands and mouth in the customary way. Slowly climbing the steps, for her strength seemed suddenly drained away, she tugged the thick rope which sounded the huge bell to arouse the deity's attention. Then, placing her hands together, she prayed earnestly to Amida for healing for little Miko-chan, as she liked to call Michiko.

She felt an added uneasiness as, with Michiko a dead weight on her back, she wearily made her way to Tajiro's home. Though he had soon followed Tazaburo to Karafuto the two brothers hadn't seen a great deal of each other's families. For one thing, they had both been fully occupied making new homes and a living in this wild, pioneer land, though Susumu did occasionally call when up there in connection with his railway duties. Taka, however, had never encouraged much visiting by the rest of the family, secretly feeling it wise for Umeno not to see much of her real father and mother since she had no longer been a baby when adopted.

Taka found the family very concerned over Tajiro's rapidly failing health, especially since Yojiro the fourth brother, who had worked at another lumber mill further away, had died not long before. So it was not a very cheerful reunion, and Taka was thankful when the time came to leave in the morning.

Michiko slept much of the way in the train, and her fever seemed a little lower. Only after the child was in bed and asleep did Taka slowly go and join the rest of the family, now anxiously waiting in the living room.

'What did the doctor say?' her husband asked hurriedly while Umeno, who had heard in the store that her mother had returned, hushed little Ichiro and strained forward to listen.

'He called it poli— poli-something. I couldn't get all those long names!' Taka sounded a little petulant. 'It's some kind of paralysis.'

'Did he give you some good medicine?' demanded Susumu.

'No. He. . . he said. . . there's no cure for it.' There was a break now in Taka's voice, and Umeno bit her lips to strangle an anguished cry.

'I doubt if he really knew what he was talking about,' Taka continued hastily. 'We'll find something that will cure her, I'm sure.'

She sounded confident but Umeno couldn't dispel the cold fear which gripped her as she remembered the two little bodies in the burying ground.

Gradually the fever subsided and Michiko was ready to be her usual active self again. But all she could do was somehow squirm over the straw mats 'like a snake' as she later described it. Fortunately she now felt no pain; but those useless, paralysed legs were forever dragging behind or getting in the way and limiting her activity severely. She could no longer sneak into the store and steal cookies for her many little friends, something which had made her very popular; but she had such a cheerful and friendly nature that other children were drawn to her anyway.

Grandma Taka didn't let any grass grow under her feet. Sometimes she would come in excitedly with news of a fortune-teller or diviner in a village a few stations down the line, and the next day she would tie Michiko on her back and off they would go. They returned with lightened purse, but no healing. Sometimes Tazaburo would hear of something at the temple and away they would go to try that remedy. And always, with more ceremony than before, they would carefully make the daily food and drink offerings to the ancestral tablets on the god-shelf in the family living room. Soon these *must* do something to improve the situation, Taka thought.

Then winter descended on the land, closing them in again, so all travel was impossible for Michiko. With the coming of spring, however, Taka kept her ears open and constantly questioned people she met. One day she came home from the fish market, her eyes sparkling.

'I've heard of an almost certain cure!' she announced. 'I met Noguchi San and she told me she knows a group of sick people who are going up to an Oroki village. Those tribal people have a great reputation for healing.'

'The Oroki!' Susumu exclaimed. 'What can *they* know about such a sickness? They can't read and even *we* had never heard of it before! I see them from the train sometimes and they're filthy-looking people. It's a waste of time to go there.'

Hearing him say this, Michiko thought he just wasn't interested in her getting well again. But her experiences of these people were to instil a fear and horror which made a lasting impression upon her.

A British traveller, Charles H Hawes, visited Sakhalin in 1901 and spent two nights in different Oroki homes of which he wrote a graphic description. Although conditions would have improved in the 35 years before Michiko met them, it probably wasn't by very much, and some were still clothed in salmon skins then.

Hawes tells us that the headman of a village came to welcome his party in answer to a gunshot from their canoe, and led them through a pack of yelping dogs to his hut. The visitors had to creep on hands and knees through the three-foot doorway and then stand half-bent to dodge the many poles fixed across the room and festooned with drying fish. A fire burned in the centre of the floor and, half-blinded by the smoke, Hawes sank onto the reindeer skin spread for him. The atmosphere was thick with the greasy smell of the fish above their heads in various stages of curing. Later he wondered if the semi-closed eyes which gave the Oroki a peculiar appearance were caused by constant smoke.

Around the fire were about twenty people of three generations. Weird-looking faces and unkempt hair would be seen a moment in the flickering blaze, then would be lost again in the darkness of the hut. Grimy brown-faced women suckled babies while taking turns smoking a Japanese pipe. Other babies were rocked violently in cradles strung from the cross poles. Children kept creeping out of corners to eye the strange visitor. The men were all devouring bits of scraggy dried fish from the same dish, and dipping them in a bowl of seal-oil.

When the men had finished the women and children ate, and rice on the children's platter proved it to be a well-to-do home. One mother having finished her meal prepared the dish for her neighbor, 'by licking it all over, drying it with a bunch of grass and finally polishing it on her gaiters'.

With the meal ended at last, the fire was banked up and all prepared for sleep by removing their skin gaiters, rolling up in another tunic and stretching out on the ground. The hut measured about 20 by 12 feet and was not only crowded, smoky and smelly, but insect-ridden as well. The Oroki were not accustomed to wash themselves and in the morning watched with great curiosity as the Englishman performed this ritual and brushed his teeth.

Michiko only remembered their homes as strange and 'round', apparently made of tree branches. Hawes says the house he was in was shaped rather like a tent — a simple scaffolding on the inside supported a horizontal pole, against which leaned a great number of larch poles from all sides, the ground plan being oval. Pieces of poplar bark served as tiles, one being shifted to the side to allow smoke to escape.

Other poles were laid on top to keep the bark in position.

Hawes was spectator the next day of a special feast inaugurating the annual sable-hunting season. The women rose early to bring in fuel, and water in bark baskets. After a hasty snack of tea and dried fish, preparations began. One woman, after scraping off the scales, put some salmon skins in a big cauldron; another pounded rice, wortle-berries and fish in a wooden trough, mixed it all with seal oil and cooked it in a little sea water. Preparations went on for hours and some of the food was then offered to the gods of the forest.

One of the various 'cures' to which Michiko was subjected on visits to the Oroki was eating food which had first been offered to their deities, and the horrible smells and strange tastes remain forever in her memory. Another 'cure' particularly abhorrent to her was eating food offered to the dead. The Oroki practice was to put their dead in boxes 'like dog houses' as she expressed it, and then place them in the forks of tree branches. When people came for healing they would open the box at one end, and to Michiko's horror the back of a head of black hair would pop out when the confining board was removed. The party of sick people were then told to worship the dead body and eat food which had been offered to it. But even this drastic measure didn't bring life back to her useless legs.

The Ainu, another tribe inhabiting Northern Japan, claimed to have a form of exorcism to cure paralysis but the Oroki form of exorcism was the most famous and the most fearsome. It was as healer of sickness, or exorcist of evil spirits, that the Sharman (similar to the medicine man of the American Indians) was most in demand. For this he tied around himself a kind of skirt attached with all kinds of jangling metal: bells, chains, metal discs, tin cans. His headdress was deer antlers from which more metal dangled.

First he burned grass in the fireplace of the house to which he was called, until it was filled with stifling blinding smoke. Then he proceed-ed to beat a big reindeer skin drum in his hand and whirled, howling, around the fireplace. The noise could reportedly be heard two miles away. Sometimes he would stop and beat himself instead of the drum, and after an hour or so his face became disfigured, his eyes horribly bloodshot, his howls hoarse yelps which, together with the rattle of all his hardware, had a terrifying effect on the watchers.

Finally exhausted, he would fling himself on the floor and fall asleep, those who sought his help having to wait until morning for the revelation he had received from the spirits. He usually prescribed the making of a wooden image of a bear or tiger, to be hung in a certain place and given offerings of fat. Other times he claimed that something the patient had done had displeased the spirits and a dog or something else of value must be sacrificed. The Sharman himself also had to be well rewarded, of course.

Michiko was probably not subjected to this treatment, but it is easy to understand her feelings of terror at the memory of the things she was exposed to as a small child, or heard from other sick people on their travels. Apart from this she really would have enjoyed the trips in the short summer months when the beauty of the mountains, the fresh green of the forests, and the ocean released from its prison of ice could all be seen from the train.

The happiest days of her early childhood were when her friends took her in a primitive little cart up the steep path to grassy fields above the cliff. There they would sit her on a rug and run back and forth bringing her daisies to make into a chain, and laugh and talk with her as if she was just like one of them. At home, by contrast, if guests were coming to the house her father would want her shut away out of sight in a closet, so as not to cause the visitors any embarrassment or discomfort.

In the spring of her sixth year a fresh gleam of hope appeared on her horizon. Her grandfather came home from the temple one day with word that a new religion had come to the island, and its leaders were setting up some kind of treatment place for the sick. This new group was called Seicho no Ie, meaning House of Growth.

Its founder didn't at first proclaim it a religion, because he believed all religions were the same and he wanted all faiths to accept his teaching. He quoted from the important scriptures of all religions, including the New Testament, pointing out where (he thought) these made wrong interpretations; he stated his purpose was to make the Christian a real Christian, the Buddhist a better Buddhist, and so on.

He claimed that while meditating on December 23rd 1928 he received from an unseen voice the following message: 'On earth there exist no sins, no sickness, no death, no poverty. Nothing in the world restrains human beings. Thou art the son of God by nature. Thou art Buddha thyself.' He realized, he said, that this voice came from heaven and he immediately wrote down the message.

His writings are prolific and most healings now are expected to come through hearing his lectures, and changing one's mental outlook. The movement's literature today is full of testimonies from people who tell of being cured from sicknesses while they listened to a lecture.

Taka Tamura knew nothing of this teaching, but if there was a chance of Michiko being cured she was ready to try anything. When Michiko heard this new place of healing was at the boom city of Susuka, the same place where they had gone for contact with the Oroki, she was filled with fear again. But nothing would deter her grandmother. So they left once more on the train and after an interview Taka was encouraged to register Michiko for treatment.

It seems that the practice in the early days of this religion must have been a little different from the present, for while Taka did have to sit and listen to endless lectures Michiko was given some very intensive massage by a therapist. Though her legs remained unchanged, the muscles of her hands and arms were developed remarkably so that at last she was able to get around fairly comfortably on some roughly-made little crutches. She has no recollection of any of the teaching, but remembers rejoicing at the enticing vista of greater independence beginning to open up before her.

Chapter Three

Sunshine and Deepening Shadow

TO THE TRADITIONAL WAY OF THINKING Michiko was an object for her family to be ashamed of, to be kept out of sight as much as possible. Public education was a fairly recent innovation, too, and it had just never occurred to her grandparents that she would ever go to school. So, as April of the year children her age began their education came and passed, Michiko watched the other children each day with increasing frustration. She eagerly enquired what they did and the more she heard the more she was sure she was quite capable of learning those things, even if she couldn't take part in all the games and physical activities. So she determined that she must go too.

At first her grandparents laughed at the idea. Then, as she persisted, they gave the reasons why it was impossible.

'How could you learn with legs like that? The teacher could never be bothered with you and others would laugh at you. It's quite impossible.'

So Michiko asked her friends to teach her some of the things they had learned, and to write some of the simpler Chinese characters which the Japanese many centuries before had borrowed and fitted to their own language. Finally one day she contrived to meet the teacher, a kindly person who was attracted by Michiko's bright, smiling face.

'It's not impossible for you to be admitted to the school,' she told her, 'provided your family will be responsible for getting you there and home again each day.'

At first her grandfather insisted it was too far and too difficult. The school was on the plateau on top of the high cliff the other side of the railway, and the way up was by a steep winding path which would often be impassable in winter. Finally, however, it was arranged that grandfather Tazaburo would take her on the back of his bicycle, the teacher would help her around during school hours and either grandfather or one of the workers at the store would fetch her at the end of the day.

So the next April Michiko went to school. Her enjoyment was unbounded, for she already had so many friends from around her home that those who came from other areas soon welcomed her too. Thus she was not only in her element mentally but was accepted socially. She felt an unending sense of wonder at the many new things she saw and heard, and thrilled at the thought that this was only the beginning!

Even when winter snows made the path to school impossible for her grandfather, the teacher came faithfully each afternoon to give Michiko an assignment to do the following day. Although feeling deep regret at having to stay home, Michiko applied herself wholeheartedly to her school work and at the end of the first winter was elated to find she had managed to keep up with her classmates.

She now not only had a new awareness of her family relationships but also of her native island. She learned that it was long and narrow, as she looked at the map on the classroom wall each day; though it had always seemed an endless expanse to her previously she learned that it varied from only 16 miles to 100 in width, but was nearly 600 miles long. Its shape was roughly like that of a sturgeon fish. Up near its northwest coast was the mouth of the huge Amur river flowing from the vast Asian mainland which was separated from the island only by the narrow Tartary Strait.

The Chinese had actually been the first to record any knowledge of the island, referring to it in the Tang dynasty as Liu Kuei Kuo (Country of Vagrant Devils). In the following Mongol dynasty the island had come under Chinese sovereignty, and although an expedition in 1264 was resisted by the Ainu inhabitants, tribute had been paid to the Chinese emperors.

For centuries, however, it had been largely left undisturbed to primitive tribes of Ainu, Oroki and Gilyak, plus a wealth of wild life. Big brown bears had roamed in large numbers and in addition there were wolves, and many foxes valuable for their red, silver and black pelts; sables were plentiful, also otters, martens and hare as well as deer and the numerous domesticated reindeer of the Orokis. There were no good natural harbors, however, and both for this reason and because of the long intensely cold winters and frequent thick fog surrounding the coast, neighboring nations had not been attracted to

the island. The fog resulted from the meeting of the warm Japan
('Black') Current and the cold waters of the Arctic, and this also
accounted for the great varieties of fish which swarmed around the
island, as well as whales and seals.

The industrial revolution, the advent of steam ships and the
rapidly expanding colonial aspirations of many western countries had
now changed the situation. American whalers had come to the surrounding islands, attracted by the great catch to be had there;
Japanese fishermen had visited the coasts in ever-increasing numbers,
while the Russian Empire was fast expanding across Siberia, taking
advantage of the growing weakness of the Manchu dynasty to seize
many of the outposts of the Chinese Empire until it finally gained
control of some of the Pacific coast.

Michiko did not know anything about the past history of the island, nor the neighboring nations, in her early life at school, but she
did soon begin to realize that the land of her birth was in fact only an
outpost, an island colony of the great Empire of Japan.

'Ojii-san,' she called to her grandfather as he dozed beside the fire
one winter morning as she studied her lessons, 'Who were the very first
people to live here in Karafuto?'

'What's that? The first people here? Why, those primitive tribes
you used to go and visit up north with Obaa-san, when she was trying
to find a cure for your legs. Do you remember?'

Remember! Would she ever be able to forget those horrors?
Michiko merely nodded.

'But they never did anything for the country. They are so ignorant.
We Japanese had to come and really develop the place.'

'Why do we call it Karafuto then, — "Place where the Chinese
people are"? I've never seen any Chinese,' Michiko said in a puzzled
voice.

'Oh, that was long, long ago. Then they grew so weak, the
Russians drove them back even from the mainland across the water.
But our Japanese fishermen have been coming here for generations.
Why, our people were the first to explore and map this island proper-
ly,' Tazaburo said proudly, 'and that was over 300 years ago now.'

Michiko found it impossible to imagine 300 years, and returned to
her studies.

Then very gradually, from remarks heard occasionally at home
and from the content of some lessons at school, she became aware that
the great and wonderful country of Japan had some vague, but
ominous enemies.

'Ojii-san, what does the 50th Parallel mean?' she asked her grandfather as they were riding home from school one day. He seemed to be staring straight ahead for a minute.

'It's one of the imaginary lines dividing up the globe — the world — parallel to the Equator, the centre of the earth. It just means being 50 degrees from the Equator,' he added.

Michiko wasn't sure how big a degree was, though she had heard the word often in connection with the cold in winter. But this wasn't the kind of answer she had expected. As her grandfather remained silent, she tried again.

'But what has it to do with us — with Karafuto, Ojii-san?' she persisted.

'We Japanese own Karafuto up to the 50th Parallel. North of that, this island is called Sakhalin, as you've heard, and the Soviets claim it now — quite wrongly of course. We Japanese discovered the island long before they did and have fished here for centuries!'

'So how did it happen — about the Parallel, I mean?' Michiko enquired anxiously.

'Oh, it's a long story. But up to fifteen years ago we owned the whole island, and would do still but for Soviet treachery!' Tazaburo spat indignantly and pedaled faster a moment to relieve his feelings.

'Our Navy had a great victory over the Russians 25 years ago when they tried to claim the island,' he finally continued. 'That was ten years before we came here, and I was still in the Army. I can remember our General announced "Sakhalin is lost to the Russians forever". But there was some trickery away over in America where the peace treaty was signed, and instead of us getting the island it was divided at the 50th Parallel, Russia being given the north with all the oil and coal, and Japan only the south. You can never trust any foreigners!'* Tazaburo spat again.

'But I thought you said it all belonged to us fifteen years ago?'

'Yes, I did. After that disgraceful peace treaty the Russians tried to settle some of their people up north, but no one wanted to come; it had such a bad name apparently, from their earlier prison colonies there. Then war broke out in Europe and later people called Bolsheviks fought the other Russians, and eventually seized the government. But earlier they killed 700 Japanese settlers on the mainland, so our forces

---

*The Japanese viewpoint was, naturally, the only one known to the Tamuras. A brief summary of the earlier history of Sakhalin is given at the end of the book (Appendix 2) to enable readers better to understand subsequent events.

seized the north of the island in retaliation — and of course it belonged
to us anyway, and we certainly didn't want any Bolsheviks here.'

'I've never heard of Bolsheviks before,' Michiko said in a puzzled
voice.

'They call themselves Communists now — it sounds better I
suppose. And all the countries the Russians seized are called the
Soviet Union today. But we had the whole island from 1920 to 1925.
Those were the days.'

'Well, what changed it?' asked the ever-curious Michiko.

'I never rightly understood it. The Soviets and Chinese signed a
Friendship Treaty in 1924 and somehow that seemed to threaten our
interests over there on the mainland. It was trade and politics all mixed
up, I expect. Anyway our government, without consulting us here in
Karafuto, signed another agreement with the Soviets, giving up our
claim to north Sakhalin but keeping our rights to develop oil, coal,
mineral and forests up there for the next 45 years.'

'So there's still another thirty years to go,' Michiko calculated.
'What will happen then?'

'Who knows? Perhaps we'll be strong enough to regain our rights,
judging by the way our armies are growing.' Her grandfather paused.
'But that's a long way off, and I won't be here to see it, and I doubt that
you will either, Miko-chan.' He shook his head sadly as they reached
their gate. There he unstrapped Michiko's crutches, then helped her
off the back of his bicycle, utterly unsuspecting how wide of the mark
his prediction would soon prove to be.

In fact much had been taking place in the world and in the
Japanese home islands which had not yet made any impact on the
people of Karafuto.

The north Sakhalin population had now risen to over 100,000.
Soon after the withdrawal of the Japanese military forces from there in
1925, shock brigades from Communist Youth organizations had come
over to build roads and houses, clear forests and set up collectivized
agricultural centers. Oil and coal production was speeded up to meet
the fuel needs of the new Soviet industrial complexes in the Amur
region. And the more firmly the Soviets were established the less they
liked the increasing Japanese efforts to develop their concessionary
rights there.

In 1936 Japan and Germany signed an Anti-Comintern Pact
against the countries in the Soviet orbit. This was hardly noticed by
the Tamura family in their distress over Michiko's devastating sickness, but it had two significant and ominous consequences. The first

was an even further cooling of relations between Japan and the Soviets, and the second a growing admiration of the new German leader, Hitler, among many of Japan's military forces and youth. In an incredibly short time, fanatical young nationalists and militants in effect overthrew Japan's democratic government and with it the freedom of the press, the militants from then on controlling all news.

The partition at the 50th parallel had literally cut the island in half. Across its 90 mile breadth a ten-meter-wide strip was cleared of all trees and shrubs, with a further short no-man's-land area on both sides. The Treaty allowed no military fortifications to be built there. Only the Oroki moved from one territory to the other on some of their hunting trips in the mountains. Japanese contacts with the north were solely by sea, as they followed up their concessions to exploit the oil and coal fields.

Michiko's father, constantly travelling, was more aware of what was going on in the world than most people in the village, as he overheard various bits of gossip or talked with other railway employees. He worked on the stretch of railway leading up the east coast almost to the 50th parallel and one day he came home with a troubled look on his face.

Ignoring Michiko's presence he began talking excitedly to her grandfather.

'The Soviets have been shooting across the border!' he exclaimed. 'They killed two of our police who were escorting a member of the Diet on a tour up there. What will our government do about it, d'you think?'

Tazaburo shook his head in perplexity and anger. 'You can never trust those Russians. They'll stop at nothing! But our government will take care of it somehow.'

Michiko, whose personal knowledge of Russians was limited to a white Russian family who had a delicious bakery in a nearby town, wondered what could be so bad about them.

A few weeks later, Susumu reported hearing that the Soviets were building military installations across the 50th parallel, completely against the terms of the Treaty. The rumor was that they were building an airfield!

Soon extra freight trains, filled with mysterious equipment, began heading north while a few Japanese naval uniforms were visible among passengers travelling in the same direction. Surreptitious rumors began to circulate that the Japanese Navy was building an airfield near Susuka, the last big town before the 50th parallel; then that the Army was building another in the south near Karafuto's capital city Toyohara.

Michiko was filled with excitement at her first glimpse of a plane, cruising so easily and gracefully through the heavens. She longed to be up in one to see the whole expanse of her island, looking so beautiful in the rare, sunny days of the brief summer.

The fog and ice of winter followed summer, and the skies became empty. Michiko was imprisoned at home again but she continued to work hard there and keep up with her classmates. She greatly missed the social life, but now that she could read easily the books in the little school library opened up a new world to her. So, apart from this temporary absence from school, she was aware of no clouds on the horizon to mar the promise of the future. All she could foresee was seven or eight more years of school with its constant revelations of new and interesting things.

Chapter Four

Ominous Rumors and Bitter Realities

ONE DAY SUSUMU RETURNED TRIUMPHANTLY from a visit to the city with a very welcome addition to the household — a radio! Michiko appreciated this especially in the long winter months. It broadened her outlook, as well as providing some entertainment, although the music consisted almost entirely of military marches.

The word 'war' was frequently heard on the news after Germany invaded Poland in 1939, but the European war seemed very far from Karafuto. Japan's invasion of China in 1937 was in quite a different category, of course — there the Japanese were said to be bringing peace and order as they progressed further and further west. Radio announcers praised the beauty and glory of Japan's 'divine mission' and the sacred war in China, while speaking increasingly harshly about the Americans and British, who were doing all kinds of evil in the world.

The Japanese government were working to build up the impression that Japan was dangerously threatened from outside — and most of them probably believed this. If Japan was to maintain its hold on Manchuria, Korea and China, military and naval forces must find new sources of oil and the Dutch East Indies, via the Philippines, was the nearest obvious supply. To reach this objective the American Pacific Fleet, based in Hawaii, would have to be eliminated, and the government considered this would be just retaliation for the anti-Japanese immigration laws passed by the USA in 1924, which had continued to rankle with patriotic and politically-minded Japanese ever since.

Most of the hard-working colonists on Karafuto understood little about these events. They merely rejoiced to hear that the Emperor's forces were bringing order, or freeing many Asian peoples from their colonial oppressors. To them the tension with the Soviets across the 50th parallel seemed much more important.

On the evening of April 14, 1941, Tazaburo's face had really broken into a smile as news came that the previous day the government had concluded a Neutrality Pact with the Soviets.

'What does that mean?' asked the ever-curious Michiko.

'It means they won't try to get any of our land, and if another country attacks us the Russians won't side with them,' her grandfather answered. 'So that's going to make everything a lot easier for us.'

But the whole agreement had not been made public — there was a secret clause stating that the Japanese would liquidate all their concessions on Sakhalin by the end of the year. The government was evidently so confident of reaching new East India sources of oil that they felt they could sacrifice the Sakhalin trickle in order to gain Soviet neutrality. Most residents of Karafuto would have been very indignant if they had known about this.

The German attack on Russia only two months later took everyone by surprise. Some in the Japanese government advocated a 'second front' push into Siberia, in spite of the newly-signed Treaty. This was soon seen to be impossible until they had the needed oil, but they did press for their drilling rights in Sakhalin to continue until 1943, and the Soviets had to agree since the German armies were almost at Moscow. So although part of the Northern Regional Army, some of Japan's most seasoned troops, were then in Karafuto, they were ordered to avoid any friction with the Russians. Instead they were deployed on road construction, and the expansion of railway and port facilities.

In December 1941 Japan destroyed the American Fleet at Pearl Harbor, bringing America into the war. Soon various rumors began to circulate that the USSR would allow the Americans to construct bases opposite Karafuto's west coast, and there were fears of a Soviet-American invasion. But news of great Japanese victories directed everyone's attention to their triumphant sweep through China, Hong Kong, Indo-China, Burma, the Malay Peninsula, the Philippines and finally New Guinea.

On Karafuto most people's days were fully occupied, however, coping with ever-increasing demands for its products. The mines, pulp mills and other industries were working at capacity while local officials continually urged people to grow more food to be self-supporting.

'Obaa-san,' Michiko said eagerly to her grandmother on returning from school one early spring afternoon, 'the teacher said that even children should be growing vegetables. I can't do much, but — could you do more if I help in some other way? They want 75,000 acres more to be cultivated.'

'I'm already growing things on every inch of our land! And no one has better vegetables. What more do they want?'

'Couldn't we keep some chickens then? I could help with those,' Michiko pleaded.

Taka finally agreed to that, and from then on Michiko really enjoyed feeding and giving names to each one, proudly noting the number of eggs they produced.

Michiko's father, who was very busy with the extension of the railway north to the new town of Koton, almost at the 50th parallel, and with the huge quantities of freight moving in both directions, came home one day looking unusually worried. As soon as Taka was out of earshot Michiko heard him speak in a low voice to her grandfather.

'It's strange! They've withdrawn the units of the Northern Regional Army up at Koton, and are replacing them with older reservists or young students. I don't like the look of things. These fellows will be no match for the Americans or the Russians.'

'Why would they do that?' Ojii-san scratched his head in puzzlement. 'Well, perhaps they know there's no danger up there now, after the Neutrality Pact.'

But Susumu didn't look convinced.

Imperceptibly at first, the radio reports of the victories of the great Imperial forces gradually grew less frequent and less detailed. Nothing was said about the serious defeats the Japanese navy had begun to experience.

Once again Susumu Tamura came in with a serious face.

'Do you know what I heard today?' he whispered to Tazaburo. 'A man who should know told me we have given up all our oil concessions in Sakhalin, and they are experimenting in the forests further down the line trying to distil gasoline from pine needles!'

'Well we have plenty of those on Karafuto! It sounds a great invention!'

'It sounds crazy to me! I just don't understand what's going on.'

Michiko thought her father always seemed to see the dark side of things. What brought the cost of the war home to her at last in a really personal and painful way was when first one, then another teacher disappeared from school and was not replaced. Finally as Michiko finished 4th grade the bitter bombshell broke: the school could not reopen because of lack of staff. The men were all needed to fight in the Emperor's army and the women to become nurses or do other necessary war work.

Michiko's grief and disappointment were almost unbearable at first. But as spring turned into early summer she had more time to observe the wonders of nature around her. She grew friendly with the tiny chipmunks, feeding them crumbs from left-overs in the store whenever she could go to the temple courtyard or the grassy patches near the shore which they frequented. She wistfully watched their quick dainty movements as they darted about, or sat holding the food in their little hand-like paws, then chewed it or stuffed it, for later use, into the pockets inside their prettily marked cheeks.

Very occasionally her friends took her in a little cart further around the bay, where they could see the great ocean breakers rolling in ceaselessly, roaring and pounding against the great cliffs. Michiko shuddered with fear as she watched, imagining being tossed helplessly in their churning depths with no hope of being able to swim.

'The waves look so powerful', she thought. 'It's surprising they haven't conquered the cliffs long ago, and overrun the island. How strong those rocks must be! They've withstood that pounding for centuries! I need to be like those firm rocks if I'm going to survive the problems of being handicapped like this.' Mercifully, the extent of those difficulties was still completely beyond her imagination.

Reassured, she would turn her eyes from the waves to the beautiful seagulls wheeling above her, or occasionally swooping down into the water to snatch some food, then gracefully floating up on a current of air to rest in some crevice high in the cliffs. How Michiko longed to have wings, instead of those wretched legs which somehow did not seem to belong to her. She enjoyed watching all the birds, especially as she began to recognize the many different species. As summer drew to an end she watched the grey geese and many varieties of duck head off in their perfect formation to warmer climes in the south; she had no idea how similar-shaped, sinister formations of Japanese planes were bringing fear, disorganization, destruction and death to thousands in China and other places.

A gloriously sunny first week in October was followed inevitably by the first snowfall, and soon they were imprisoned by winter again. As usual, Michiko had to spend most of her time by the fire, for if she was too long out on a sled her feet might freeze without her realizing it. But she continued to practise writing the intricate Japanese characters, and also helped Ichiro a little since there was no school for him either. Miyoko, the baby sister who had come to join the family some months before, was getting to be more of a companion too.

Other changes in the family were not so happy, however. Soon after they heard that uncle Tajiro had died, grandfather Tazaburo had another slight heart attack, giving them all great concern. He gradually gained strength again, but Michiko's mother had been extra busy without his assistance in the store, and other help was almost impossible to get now. Her father too always seemed to be working overtime on the railway.

Michiko now listened to the radio more than ever with her grandfather. One day they, together with many others on Karafuto, heard that the Russians had finally stopped the German army at Stalingrad and had now begun to push them back westward. But this was far, far away, and seemed of little consequence to the people of Karafuto.

They could not have been more terribly mistaken! In February 1945 a triumphant Stalin met with Winston Churchill and Franklin Roosevelt at Yalta. In a secret agreement with them he promised that within two or three months of the total defeat of Germany he would declare war on Japan (in spite of the Treaty of Neutrality with them) and would attack from Siberia and north Sakhalin. The price Stalin demanded from the allies for this help was the restoration of all Russian rights 'violated by the treacherous attack of Japan in 1904', among which was the return of sovereignty over south Sakhalin and the Kuriles.*

Japan of course knew nothing about this, and went on trusting to the Neutrality Pact which was valid for another year.

But in the early spring a new word began to be heard — invasion. It was rumored that the Americans would try to invade the Kuriles or Karafuto, and everyone must be prepared to defend the island. Though no hint of this appeared in the newspaper or on the radio, Susumu came home one day with some information which he knew was no rumor.

'There are train-loads of the 88th Division troops being moved south,' he told his father. 'It's hard to believe there can be any men left

---

*This would break the Portsmouth Treaty of 1905, the Soviet-Japan Convention of 1925 and the Neutrality Pact of 1941, each of which directly or indirectly confirmed Japanese sovereignty in Karafuto. But Roosevelt and Churchill were so anxious to end the war quickly that they either didn't care or didn't take the trouble to find out how their new agreement would negate past treaties.

up there. But no replacements seem to be moving up to the 50th parallel! I just don't understand it.'

While they heard nothing officially of any reverses on Japan's far-flung battle fronts, rumors somehow began to circulate. A railway friend returning to Mototomari told Susumu that Japanese were begin-ning to arrive in Karafuto's capital saying their homes on the mainland had been bombed flat by American planes, and they had come to seek safety.

The Soviets announced on April 9 that the Neutrality Pact was to terminate, but foreign minister Molotov assured the Japanese govern-ment this merely signified that it would expire naturally in 1946 and would not be renewed.

In May, Japan's ally Germany finally capitulated.

On June 6 a U.S. submarine fired on an island about a hundred miles out to sea from Mototomari, and from then on events moved swiftly to their dreadful climax of fire, detention or death for the majority of the inhabitants of Karafuto.

News came on the 12th of a freighter having been torpedoed in Aniwa Bay, a hundred miles south of Mototomari, and in succeeding days several ships exploded around the coast of Karafuto. To prevent further losses, the government on July 7 made the fateful decision to halt the ferry to Hokkaido, thus cutting off Karafuto completely from the rest of Japan.

All this still seemed remote from Michiko, but a day later her father came bursting in from the station with more news.

'A freight train was blown up on the line this morning! They say some American commandos landed from submarines last night and placed demolition charges on the track near Shirahama!'

This was very much closer to home! The first time Michiko heard the weird, penetrating wail of the air-raid siren it seemed to set every nerve of her body tingling, although she knew it was only a practice warning. By now all able-bodied civilians were being drafted to emer-gency defence work, and many began digging air-raid shelters for protection against possible American bombing. Retired soldiers and young students formed volunteer guard units, but no arms were avail-able.

August came, with dark premonitions of impending disaster, but when it struck its source was a complete surprise to most of the civilian population of Karafuto. Unknown to them, all through June the lookouts on duty among the mere 4,000 men left as defence at the 50th parallel had seen considerable activity on the Soviet side. They had also noted most elaborate efforts to camouflage the operations.

The chief of staff of the 88th Division sent repeated warnings to military headquarters in Hokkaido through June and July, but received no response. On August 3 he notified them that a Soviet attack was imminent and put his men on full alert.

Most civilians barely noticed the radio announcement that on August 6 Hiroshima had been hit with a specially powerful bomb; after all, the big American B-29s had been pounding Japan since November, and in March and April there had been the great fire bomb raids on Tokyo itself, which had caused such terrible devastation. Far more important seemed the completely unexpected message two days later from the Soviet Union to the Japanese government, declaring that a state of war would exist between the two countries on the following day.

This news was cabled to Toyohara, the Karafuto capital, at 7 a.m. the next day — leaving little time to warn the small group left at the 50th parallel and none to warn the 450,000 civilian population.

Ever since Germany's capitulation in May, Soviet troops had been pouring east across Siberia, ready for a final overwhelming offensive against Japan. A million and a half men, thousands of planes and tanks and hundreds of destroyers, submarines and transports were ready to be thrown into a simultaneous attack on Manchuria, Korea and Sakhalin, while the United States was battering the main islands of Japan.

At Koton, the northern terminus of the railway from Mototomari, the 4,000 Japanese troops were amazingly able to withstand the 35,000 Soviet assault force for eight days. Cloudy weather and difficult terrain hindered the Russians from maximum use of their air power and armored columns.

Nagasaki's atomic bombing on the 9th passed unnoticed up north, while on the 10th officials met in Toyohara to discuss, for the first time, plans to evacuate Karafuto civilians to the mainland. A stampede began to the main ports of Maoka, Honto and Otomari, and all available ships, rowboats and even canoes were commandeered. On the same day other Soviet troops attacked fishing villages on both the east and west coasts near the 50th parallel, and the following day Soviet bombers struck several large towns, turning them into blazing infernos.

Michiko was the only one in the Tamura family who had time to listen to the radio in the midst of all this turmoil. It was she who first heard that a very important announcement was to be made to the whole Japanese nation at noon on August 15. Finally everyone became aware of it, and as the appointed hour drew near as many as possible prepared to listen, either at home or at their place of work.

A feeling of great awe prevailed when they learned it was Emperor Hirohito himself who would address them. The vast majority had never seen him, nor even heard his voice. In his brief statement he declared that in order to bring to an end any further terrible devastation of their country the government would now agree to the Allied forces' demand that Japan make an unconditional surrender. The war was therefore at an end. In conclusion he counselled them bravely to 'bear even with the unbearable'.

To the majority of the listeners it seemed utterly incredible and they were dazed and speechless for a moment. Throughout its long history Japan had never known a real military defeat and had never tasted the horrors of an invading army. Although on the main islands some committed suicide, and many were hysterical with chagrin, most had a feeling of intense relief that at least the terrible destruction and shortage of food would end. On Karafuto, disbelief, dismay, confusion and horror filled many hearts and minds, and for a few hours a deathly calm ensued as people waited for directions from the authorities.

The next day Soviet amphibious forces landed on the west coast a little north of the important rail center of Esutoru. It took them two days to fight their way into the town because the Japanese there resisted fiercely, apparently not believing that the war was over. Casualties were heavy on both sides and the Soviets executed the mayor and police chief, while 170 civilians committed suicide.

News of this quickly reached Michiko's father via the railway telegraph system, and shortly afterwards came word of the Soviet breakthrough at Koton to the north of them. Hastily a meeting was called of each neighborhood group in Mototomari.

The consensus of the one the Tamuras belonged to was that they should leave at once while the ports were still open and the trains running. Since Susumu himself was a railway worker, and had a sick father and a crippled daughter, it was expected he would have some pull. He quickly telegraphed to his brother Tajiro's remaining family, advising them also to leave at once.

A south-bound train was due in about four hours, and they decided to go on that. Hastily they began to throw things together. Some families thought it best to destroy everything in their homes, but the Tamuras knew this was impossible with the store and big house, as well as months of supplies. One thing they must do, however. They could not leave the godshelves to be desecrated by some Soviet soldier. With a sense of fear and real loss Michiko and her grandmother watched as grandfather Tazaburo reverently removed the statue of Amida, the flowers, candles, and food and incense containers from their place of honor in the big living room and took them out into the yard to burn. Only the ancestral tablets, thin pieces of wood which would be easy to carry, were left.

As her mother and grandmother hurriedly brought small items for her to tie up into convenient bundles, Michiko's feeling of emptiness and loss remained. Amida, the Buddhist deity, and the spirits of the ancestors had always been there in the house watching over the family and protecting them. Would they now be able to help on this dangerous journey?

The moment came when they must leave, though there was much more they longed to do. Grandfather led the procession, followed by the others carrying as many bundles as they could manage. The station was already jammed with people frantically trying to buy tickets, but Susumu had his pass and was able to push his way in when the train came. It was already full when it left Mototomari, and it still had over a hundred miles to go to Toyohara where they would have to change trains for the big port of Otomari. Further crowds of refugees tried to board the train at every station, and it was a desperately uncomfortable journey for everyone.

At last they reached the port from which 30,000 people had already left Karafuto; it was now packed with others awaiting passages. Susumu had telephoned ahead and been promised places on one of the ferries leaving the next evening.

Comforted by the assurance of transportation the next day, the Tamura family and others from their neighborhood followed the advice of a railway official, and camped out in some of the many empty houses on the outskirts of Otomari, vacated by families who had already left for the mainland. It was an odd feeling, taking over the home of a complete stranger, but they were very thankful for a night's rest after the terrible train journey.

Next day they gathered up their things and set out for the harbor, grandfather carrying Michiko on his back when she was weary of using her crutches. There in the distance, very prominent among a mass of smaller craft, they could see anchored the big ferry boat on which they were to sail later in the day. What a welcome sight! Michiko and the other two children became quite excited at the thought of the voyage, though the adults were still numb with dismay at all they had had to leave, and at the uncertainty of the future.

Only a few moments after the children's excited outburst on first seeing the ship, there was a sudden flash of light; a second later their eardrums were tortured with the impact of a big explosion. Then they could see a number of smaller boats approaching the harbor. Susumu let out an anguished groan.

'What's the matter?' asked Taka sharply.

'Those are Russian landing craft.'

Even as they watched, the ferry boat listed. Then, before their horrified gaze, it slowly began to sink beneath the waters of the harbor. Their last possible link with the homeland was now gone.

Chapter Five

Soviet Occupation

A SHUDDER OF APPREHENSION surged through the thousands of refugees milling around the harbor as the Russian landing craft approached. A later Soviet report described them as 'down-trodden masses craning their necks to greet the liberators' but also, rather inconsistently, added that they took 18,320 prisoners there.

The Japanese Supreme Command in Tokyo had already issued orders for all their forces to lay down arms, so no resistance was offered and the Soviets landed peacefully in Otomari. It was quite a different story at Maoka on the west coast, Karafuto's most important port since it was ice-free most of the year. There the Russian landing craft were met with a little small-arms fire from unidentified assailants along the shore, and they supposed it was organized resistance. Apparently there were a few units who either had not heard the cease-fire order, or just didn't believe it. Consequently the Russians started shooting, too, and their warships began bombarding Maoka. When Japanese peace envoys tried to approach they were cut down, and aerial attack was added, starting many fires. Atrocities were committed on both sides. Finally 1,000 lay dead. About 3,000 refugees struggled painfully across swamps, virgin forest and the dividing mountain range to Toyohara, only to be told on arrival by the Soviets now entrenched there to return to Maoka the way they had come.

The Tamura family fortunately had not yet reached the crowded harbor area of Otomari when the Russians landed, and without waiting to see further action they hastily retreated to the house where they had spent the night. Others of their group joined them there, as well as a few refugees from nearby houses, to try to decide what to do next. Some of the men counselled committing joint suicide, as many others were reported to be doing around them. But Taka Tamura in particular was against such an idea. With two healthy grandchildren now, besides Michiko, she felt there was still much to live for. So they withdrew from the others to await further developments, hopeful that the Russians would eventually allow them to leave.

City officials meanwhile met the Soviet Commander, who ordered all refugees to return home and civilian men to continue their regular work. Soviet warships then effectively sealed off La Perouse Strait, preventing any possibility of return to the Japanese mainland.

It was some days before trains could run regularly again, particularly as Soviet planes had bombed the station at Toyohara, inflicting heavy casualties on the crowds of refugees there. Susumu was ordered to leave immediately, to help get the train service operating again. At last the time came for the rest of the family to leave, and Michiko felt what a burden she must be to her grandfather in the difficult task of getting from one train to the other across the bombed area of Toyohara. The sight of an occasional dead body still lying around added to the horror of the journey. The trains were almost as crowded as when they came down, so it was a great relief when they finally arrived back at Mototomari station. But what would they find at home?

Somewhat fearfully they opened the door, and were thankful to find everything as they had left it. How they regretted now the hasty destruction of the godshelves and their equipment! But if their home was much the same, their community certainly was not. Many houses remained empty and they had no news of what had happened to the occupants except those known to have committed suicide.

One of the first things the Soviet Occupation Commander had done was to order the confiscation of all arms, automobiles and radios, and he had also banned the publication of Karafuto's one newspaper. This lack of any definite knowledge of what was going on either in their own island, or anywhere else in the world, was an unsettling, nerve-wracking experience and for Michiko, too, the radio was a particular personal loss in other ways.

Since Mototomari was over a hundred miles both from the capital and from the 50th parallel, and since there was no harbor suitable for anything bigger than a small fishing boat, Soviet forces were some time in reaching their village. So the fear and uncertainty about what still lay ahead for them was particularly unnerving. Probably due to wishful thinking, it soon began to be rumored that Moscow was going to create an 'autonomous Japanese region' similar to the Finnish area in the European part of the Soviet Union.

Finally Michiko's father came home one evening with the news that Soviet troops were expected the next day, and while apprehension increased it was almost a relief that they would now soon know the worst. Some looting was certain to take place, as was common with most occupying forces, and Soviet soldiers particularly had very little they could call their own. So the Tamuras made what preparations they could. By placing bookshelves and a desk against a wall with a large concealed closet, they were able to make a secret room in which they could hide valuables, and also the children, when the Russians came.

At last the dreaded moment arrived. There was a peremptory banging on the door with the butt of a rifle and Taka opened it to find five Soviet soldiers standing there. One remained at the door, gun in hand, while the others burst into the house and hurriedly picked up all they could carry. An hour later another group came, and so it continued for a number of days. They never came in groups of less than three. After lining the adults up against a wall and sometimes stripping them naked in search of valuables they might be hiding, one would stand guard over them while the rest rifled through drawers and closets. Anything red seemed specially to appeal to them, a particular favorite being the red under-kimono commonly worn by Japanese women then. As the weather got colder they would also come and chop up anything they fancied for fuel.

Because the Tamuras had been well-to-do and had a large house and family now, it took some time for it to be denuded in this way, especially as there were a number of unoccupied houses around, full of many of the former owners' possessions.

Susumu, through his work with the railway, had official contacts with the local Occupation force and soon realized the best thing would be to establish friendly relations with them. The soldiers were, after all, just lonely young men far from home. Accordingly, he began to invite some of them to the house in the evening. They had a very large room which in the past had been borrowed for wedding receptions and other functions, and here a number would come and play their guitars and balalaikas, and sing their traditional folk songs.

Soon officers began to be billeted in the neighboring empty houses, and after that the rougher enlisted men no longer came pillaging. Umeno even offered to do the laundry for some of the officers, thus earning their goodwill.

The Soviet government eventually decided to settle Karafuto with some of its own multi-racial peoples, and after three months the first families began to arrive in Mototomari. They were all very poor and carried whatever possessions they had in a grain sack over their shoulders. A few Japanese were still resisting in some places, so at first these unarmed newcomers were very fearful of all Japanese, and some tried to get Japanese children as kind of hostages to ensure they themselves would not be harmed.

Michiko had felt very lonely since her return home, for there were now only six other Japanese children in their large village. So when she saw there were children in these new families she wanted to go at once and make friends. At first her grandmother refused, but gradually Michiko got to know some of them. Before long they were wheeling her around in her little cart, while she showed them where to go by means of gestures. The biggest and most private play areas were in the grounds of the deserted Buddhist temples and Shinto shrines. The priests had all disappeared from the village, and the settlers' children gleefully helped themselves to the brass candlesticks and other utensils from the Buddhist altars, for their families were woefully short of household goods. Michiko admitted later that she 'told all sorts of lies' to cover up for these children when Japanese adults began to ask questions. None of the children spoke Japanese, but Michiko began to learn a little Russian to become better friends with them.

Some of the Soviet parents would be away all week working, just leaving their children alone at home, and Michiko even invited one or two to sleep at her house.

It was during this time that she first heard the word 'Christmas' which, surprisingly, proved a horrifying experience and left a fearful impression in her mind for a long time.

One family she had become friendly with invited her for a special celebration they called 'Christmas'. About ten people were there, four of them children, and Michiko was the only Japanese. After a good deal of drinking of some very potent brew, which was served to the children also, they gave each other small gifts. All the Soviet women wore earrings — perhaps they were from one of the Siberian racial groups rather than Russians — and they now gave a pair of these to Michiko.

At first she was delighted at receiving a present, then suddenly realized it would involve piercing her ears. Others saw the situation too and one man, now quite drunk, called to the woman of the house to bring a big needle. Holding it out in front of him as he staggered towards Michiko, he laughed and shouted, 'We'll soon fix it!' while motioning to the other men to come and help.

For a second Michiko froze with fright. Then flinging herself down, she somehow managed to slither under a bed in the room and rolled to the farthest corner against the wall, screaming in terror.

At last the men desisted, and the women assured Michiko everything was all right, and they would leave her alone. But she never forgot that experience, which was her only concept of Christmas for many years to come.

It was a difficult winter for everyone in Karafuto. The island had never been agriculturally self-sufficient, and with the violent outbreak of war in August some harvests had been lost and other food supplies destroyed in the bombings of the bigger cities. The Soviets introduced a rationing system but supplies were very inadequate. Theft was rife; the Tamuras lost a great deal as Japanese, Soviets and some of the thousands of Koreans who had been brought to work in the mines and concessions of north Sakhalin, all stole from their warehouses.

When the Soviets first occupied Karafuto they had ordered all civilians to return to their work, and only military men above the rank of colonel were arrested and flown off to unknown destinations in Siberia, or labor camps in north Sakhalin's mines and forests. Government bureaucrats, company managers, judges, publishers, all at first were retained as advisers to the incoming Soviet administrative personnel, who even kept the neighborhood associations as a useful tool for maintaining law and order.

Former bureaucrats now found themselves taking a census, administering food rationing, issuing identification papers or just sitting in their former offices wondering what would happen next.

In late September some schools had opened again, with a new curriculum omitting instruction in morals, history and geography; and teachers were told to introduce the fundamentals of Marxist-Leninist doctrine into the classroom. In Mototomari, however, there were not enough children for a Japanese school; later one was established only for the new settlers, to Michiko's great regret.

A newspaper appeared in October, but *Pravda* editorials and Communist propaganda articles on far-off production wonders soon bored the Japanese and they no longer read it.

On November 7 they were supposed to enjoy their first celebration of Russia's Revolution but, again, the majority of Japanese clung to their own old traditions and festivals and felt they had little to celebrate in the circumstances. Such feelings were soon more than justified. December 6 saw the first interrogations of former officials

and community leaders who were now assisting the Soviet adminis-
trators. Four days later many were arrested as 'war criminals', sen-
tenced as guilty of 'anti-Soviet activities' and sent to Siberia.

The final blow for many of the older people came on the last day
of the year when the name 'Karafuto' was abolished, and orders issued
that henceforth the entire island was to be called Soviet Sakhalin.

To Michiko the change of name meant little, but she sympathized
with her grandparents in their deep distress at losing the name of the
land for whose development they had given the best part of their lives.
New Year's Eve and the following two or three days, usually the most
important Japanese family festival, could that year hold no joy for
most of them. Even the traditional rice cakes were hard to come by,
for little rice could be grown on Karafuto, and since the Soviet navy
blocked the Strait there could be no imports from Japan.

As the family finished its simple meal of traditional noodles,
symbolic of long life, on New Year's Eve, grandfather Tamura sat back
and surveyed his family, his eyes finally resting on Susumu.

'Unless we can begin importing again soon, there's no way we can
continue the store. What with all the thefts, and missing the August
orders from the mainland, our supplies are almost gone.' His voice
sounded thin, his face looked drawn. It was a bitter moment for one
whose business acumen had always known what to stock, and when.
Now, through no fault of his own, he was beaten.

'I know,' Susumu answered hastily, 'and there's no word at the
railway offices of any private freight being approved yet. But don't
worry. If I'm kept in this job my salary will be enough for us to
manage.'

'What's the use of money if there's nothing to buy?' Tazaburo
asked petulantly. 'If *I* can't supply food for this village, who can?' he
added, with a touch of his old pride.

'Well, the Soviets will, in some form or another. That's what
Communism is all about,' his son answered dryly. 'But it won't be the
quality we've been used to.'

'Soviets!' Grandfather Tamura almost spat the word, and his son
hissed an involuntary 'Sshhh!' as he glanced around to be sure they
couldn't be overheard.

'It's better not to mention them, Father, even here at home. And I
suspect some things are going to get worse, rather than better, even
though we don't starve.'

'How can they be worse?' broke in Taka. 'Here we are having lost
our name, and with a New Year without a temple to go to, or temple

bells to ring in the New Year! But we won't starve. I have enough potatoes, carrots and radish stored away to last us through the winter, so long as they are not stolen by those Soviets or rascally Koreans.'

'Why don't you like them?' Michiko asked in perplexity. 'Some of them are nice and friendly. They're just people, the same as we are. And they don't have any food because they've just come here, and could not grow any. Some of them didn't even want to come, they told me.'

'Be quiet!' snapped her father, and her grandmother hastily intervened.

'You don't know what you are talking about, Miko-chan. It may be some of those here are not so very bad, but it's the leaders who are causing all the trouble.'

'I know one thing — I cannot take this kind of life any longer!' Tazaburo brought his fist down on the low table with surprising force. 'I'm going to the authorities to ask to be sent back to Japan. I'm too old and sick to be any use to them. And when they see Miko-chan they won't want to keep her here, either.'

Michiko winced inwardly as she heard this, and since she had known no other life she wasn't sure if she wanted to leave Sakhalin, even under the Soviets. But she knew it would be wiser to remain silent just now.

'There is no way they will release me at present,' her father said with finality. 'But if you want to go, why not try?'

Umeno looked anxiously from her father to her husband, and then at the children. What would be the plan for her? She had just begun to suspect she was pregnant again, and was very thankful she had managed to secrete some cases of canned milk in the hidden closet. Soon the conversation turned to other things.

Heavy snow and icy winds kept Michiko and her grandfather indoors for the next month or two. They managed to live off Taka's potatoes, but there was no more flour or sugar for her mother to make the cookies to sell. In March a new blow struck. Their familiar Japanese yen currency was withdrawn and replaced with roubles, which made Michiko's grandparents grumble endlessly.

When spring finally came towards the end of May, Tazaburo determined to go to Toyohara, the capital, to apply for repatriation. He had already been to the local official, but guessed he had little power in such things.

So one morning in early June they set out to the station with Michiko tied on her grandfather's back, and Taka carrying a little food for the two-day trip. As they approached, a further shock awaited them. A man was painting a new sign on the station board. Instead of the familiar name *Mototomari,* there was a strange-looking Russian name, spelled out in Japanese characters, VOSTOCHNYI!

'What are they going to do next!' grandfather muttered to Susumu who had just come from the station office to see them on the train. 'It is our country! What right have they to change that?'

'Quiet!' came an urgent whisper from his son. 'You mustn't talk like that in Toyohara, or you may find yourself in prison. And don't forget to take off your hat when you go into the official's office. Don't you remember hearing that all place names were to be changed on June 1st?' he added.

His father had heard, of course, but somehow he had thought that was just for the benefit of the Russians and that both names would be there. For him it could only be Mototomari. But could it, he wondered now. Perhaps you would even have to use the hated new word to get a train ticket! He shook his head in utter dismay as they passed station after station with all the familiar names gone. He hardly knew where he was!

At last they reached Toyohara, and finally arrived at the right government office. Grandfather was now breathless with the exertion, but he remembered to remove his hat. Then he untied the cloth which held Michiko on his back, and let her down so that her legs were fully visible. He greeted the official with great formality, and then continued, 'You see that we have such a child as this. She will be useless for any work in the future. I, too, have had several severe heart attacks, and have a deep desire to return to my ancestral home to die, and my wife, too. We wish to apply for repatriation to Japan.'

Michiko again cringed inwardly at being exposed thus to this stranger, but she smiled at him and he didn't look too unfriendly.

'There are no official plans yet for repatriation,' he said. 'But keep in touch with us and as soon as any changes come in the regulations your case will be considered.'

As they left the office building Taka Tamura stopped.

'Let's go back down the Jinja Dori (Shinto Shrine Street) and see what it looks like now, shall we?'

Her husband nodded agreement, although it meant a little further to walk. As they entered the capital's main thoroughfare they saw it, too, had a new name. It was now Karl Marx Street.

Soon they were in front of Karafuto's most important shrine to the Sun goddess, supposed ancestor of Japan's imperial family. Here

Tazaburo Tamura had witnessed the visit of the Emperor, then Crown Prince, in the early days of its construction. Now it stood empty, dirty and neglected. A notice carried the information that the new administration proposed eventually turning it into a planetarium.

What did it all mean? What were the deities doing to allow their descendants to suffer such humiliating disgrace and cruel hardships? At that moment of confrontation, unknown to his wife and Michiko, the first tiny seed of doubt was sown in the heart of this loyal son of traditional Japan.

Chapter Six

Nightmare Journey

THE SUMMER ADVANCED, with no news of any repatriations. Grandmother had planted her garden as usual, and had a good crop of potatoes, carrots, turnips, cabbages and cucumbers. Some of Michiko's Soviet friends were still very short of food, and so she showed them where Taka's garden was and they would happily pull some of the vegetables and eat them raw, on the spot.

Once her grandmother appeared unexpectedly to do some weeding and the children raced for their lives as Taka tried to chase them, angrily waving her hoe. Michiko, who couldn't run away, had to bear the brunt of the scolding.

'Fool! Fool! Why do you let these rascals come and steal our food? They will just grow up into thieves, like their parents who have stolen our country! Haven't you any sense?'

'But they were so hungry,' was all Michiko could say in self-defence. Then she added wistfully, 'And they are the only friends I have.'

'Nonsense! What about Ichiro and Miyoko? And next week — probably — there will be the new baby! That will give you plenty to do!'

As she remembered this wonderful event Taka's anger suddenly evaporated and she attacked the weeding with great vigor, wanting to have plenty of good food for Umeno, and eventually the new baby.

In due time the family welcomed a baby boy, whom they named Shooji.

On the mainland, meanwhile, various groups were beginning to petition the U.N. Occupation Authorities in Tokyo, asking them to intervene in Moscow on behalf of Japanese residents of former colonies now held by the Soviets. In fact, over 2½ million Japanese military and civilian personnel were known to have been captured in Manchuria, North Korea, Karafuto and the Kuriles.

Finally, one glorious day in mid-October 1946, Soviet authorities in Karafuto announced that a first group of 30,000 people might return to Japan after November. During the next two years almost 250,000 were ferried from Maoka to the west coast of Hokkaido. In the busy summer months 3,000 a day were loaded on two dilapidated steamers, 'overflowing with a grey mass of material and human baggage' as one observer described it.

The Tamuras were not accepted among those first 30,000 but they were not sorry — the winter journey would have been difficult with a young baby. Finally, after many petitions, their name was put down for a steamer leaving late July, 1947.

Michiko's feelings were a mixture of excitement and apprehension as she heard her mother and grandmother discuss the preparations for the journey: what to take and who should carry what. She had entered her teens now and was well aware of the burden she would be. Her father had been refused a pass, as he was still required on the railway. That meant they would be a party of seven, three adults and four children counting herself. Grandfather was to carry her when necessary; her mother would have little Shooji, now quite heavy but not walking, plus all that he needed. Grandmother would carry food for the other six, for the three days they expected it to take before they were on the ship. Ichiro and Miyoko would carry what little they could.

'We'll have to wear all we possibly can,' Umeno said. 'There's no way we can take even a change of clothes for everyone,' and she sighed deeply.

'Don't fret about that. From what I hear, most people don't have much left by the time they reach the boat, anyway,' her husband remarked.

'What do you mean?'

'Oh, that's just what I heard,' he answered vaguely, then hurriedly added, 'and the ships are so crowded, there isn't room for much luggage.'

'Well, the clothes we have left are so old, they're hardly worth taking,' said Taka, perhaps already envisaging buying new outfits for all when they got back to the homeland. She little realized what conditions were still like there.

Michiko's mother looked a little worried but said nothing further.

At last the day came when they must leave the house which had been home for so many years. They had longed to leave so often, yet tears were near the surface for all of them.

The farewell to Susumu at the station was sad too — would they ever see him again? Michiko herself hardly felt she would miss him much, for she still sometimes found it hard to believe he was her father. She did wonder how they were going to live when they got to Japan, though, for her grandfather certainly wouldn't be able to work.

The train was nearly full when it arrived and they were only able to get three seats between them. They had never experienced a train ride like it before. Many of the passengers going to be repatriated had brought all the luggage they could possibly carry, most of them having a big suitcase-shaped double basket which they could fix by straps across their shoulders. Soon the aisles and compartments were littered with these, and it was hard to move at all.

The worst thing, however, was that the train didn't only stop at stations. It would frequently come to a halt for no apparent reason and the train driver and a number of Soviet soldiers would come walking through the coaches holding out their hats, intimating that the train would not proceed further until everyone had made a contribution of money or jewelry.

They had to change at Manue into the train to take them over the mountains to Maoka, the big port on the west coast. On the second night Michiko remembers the train stopping in the dark at a very steep hill. Probably it was at the pass over the top of the mountain range, and perhaps the train had to be lightened somewhat to make the grade. At any rate, they were all forced to alight from the train with all their belongings, and hurry up this steep hill. Many just could not make it with their baggage, which they had to abandon at the wayside to waiting Russians.

At the top of the hill they were all forced to walk through a narrow door, and here again, any who could not get through carrying their luggage had to leave it behind.

Michiko was very fearful during this steep climb in the darkness, for the way was rough, making it very difficult for her grandfather to carry her, and his asthmatic wheezing was painful to hear. Yet it was impossible for her to go on crutches up that steep path in the dark. Many little children were crying from being disturbed in their sleep and some seemed to get lost. Taka kept Ichiro with her, while Umeno with Shooji on her back, held Miyoko's hand; but when they were finally allowed back on the train Michiko was horrified to notice that some of the children of other passengers seemed to be missing.

From the time they left home on this harrowing journey it took three days and nights to cover the less than 150 miles to the port. Many had now lost most of their belongings, and few had much money left after the constant visitations of the soldiers. They thankfully crawled from their cramped quarters on the train, believing that the worst must surely now be over.

Disillusionment soon followed. They were told that their ship would be delayed several days for repairs, and everyone was to be billeted in an empty school. This was crowded with bunk beds on which were *tatami* straw mats as mattresses, while further mats filled the floor space. Often more than eight people, with their luggage, had to share one mat no larger than six feet by three, so there was no space to lie down. Fortunately, as it was summer, they could walk around outside most of the time. Their food was almost gone, but the Soviet authorities provided soup and a small amount of bread each day.

The cramped quarters, and inevitable reaction to the disappointment of not getting away after months of hardship, suffering and impatient waiting, were just too much for some of the people, and a few went crazy. To cope with this, the authorities produced a cage-like wooden structure in which these unfortunate mental cases were locked, in public view of the other refugees. Some even jeered at them and teased them, to relieve the monotony of those dreary, uncomfortable days.

The week dragged to its weary end, and at last their ship was ready. Certainly no pleasure cruise awaited them. It was a rusty old boat and was soon loaded down with its complement of shabby passengers.

Some just stood on the deck looking stunned, weary-eyed and aged as the ship pulled away from the dock. Most settlers were leaving with a mixture of relief and regret. They had spent years creating a home out of the wilderness, only to lose almost everything in a few terrible weeks. Yet the majority happily anticipated getting back to the homeland and away from their Soviet masters. Although they knew things couldn't be easy after the long drain of war, most had no conception of the vast destruction resulting from the many bombings; and although some had no idea where they could live or find work, at least they felt they would be free from the hated Russians and their alien language.

Some did not even realize that Japan was under the control of alien Occupation forces, though a very few had heard rumors that the Americans were not as offensive as the Russians. In fact there was little pillage or rape, for American soldiers were well paid and could buy cheaply in their own stores things that were absolute luxuries to the Japanese after seven years of extensive and costly warfare.

The policy of the Allied Powers, and General Douglas MacArthur in particular, was enlightened reform, rather than retaliation and retribution. In their view the defeat of Japan and Germany had solved all the major problems of the world, and all that was needed was the reform of the culprits. Initially it was thought this would require drastic measures, but the Japanese were so used to obeying authority that the large majority cooperated willingly, accepting the American reforms with the same unquestioning faith they had shown in their former leaders.

People were bewildered and disillusioned with the leadership of the militarists, whose program of 'prosperity through conquest' had not only lost their whole empire but brought death, devastation and economic ruin to the homeland. To most Japanese, MacArthur was now the symbol of hope, a strong leader who saw with confidence beyond the destruction and despair of defeat to a brighter, better Japan of the future.

While all military officers, Diet members and high-ranking bureaucrats had been dismissed and barred from public office, none were sent to labor camps and comparatively few to prison and execution. Some would actually be restored to public life before the end of the Occupation.

Though news of it had not reached the Tamuras before they left Sakhalin, a new Constitution had been adopted on May 3rd. This defined the position of the Emperor as merely the symbol of state and of the unity of the people. He derived from the will of the people, in whom would reside sovereign power. The Diet was to be the highest organ of state, rather than the Cabinet, bureaucracy, or military forces as formerly, and it was also to be the sole law-making body. The peerage was abolished and the electorate widened to include all adult women.

Among those who boarded the ferry with Michiko and her family, however, there were probably few who would have been very interested, even had they known about the new Constitution. For most, it would seem of less importance than the urgent need for food, work and housing. As soon as the ship passed out of the harbor into the open sea, however, thoughts of the future faded abruptly as the unaccustomed motion proved too much for the majority; they succumbed to seasickness for the rest of the voyage to Hakodate, the main port on Hokkaido.

Here the Tamuras, and in fact most of the refugees, had to tranship for Honshu, Japan's main island. They planned to go to the family farm in Kominato to begin with, and so needed a ferry to the port of Aomori.

At this point Michiko experienced one of the most terrible moments of her life. They had to go in a lighter to board the ferry, and then climb up by an unsteady rope ladder. Once more Michiko was hoisted on her grandfather's back, and the supporting cloth tied around his waist. With each step up the swaying ladder his breathing became more labored, and Michiko heard him muttering, 'I can't get up, — I can't make it......' Then, horror of horrors, she felt his fingers begin to untie the cloth that held her safely against his back!

As they lurched sideways on the swinging ladder, Michiko's eyes caught sight of the dark, swirling water below, and her previous fear of being tossed in the crashing waves against the cliffs near Mototomari flashed through her mind. Without the cloth around her she knew she hadn't strength to hold on with her hands, while her useless legs swung crazily with every lurch of the rope ladder.

'Is Ojii-san going to throw me away now, as those other children were abandoned along the way?' she wondered.

She heard his gasp again. The fingers of his right hand were still fumbling with the first knot in the cloth, while with the other hand he clung precariously to the rope ladder.

Then, miraculously, a hand pushed Michiko up from below, easing the weight on her grandfather, while another arm reached down from above to help pull him up. After days of struggle on the train and in the school, with each fighting for his own survival, this help was unexpected, and relief flooded Michiko's heart. But the stark horror experienced in that moment she was suspended perilously over the dark waters of the harbor remains still vivid in her memory.

Even on board this vessel their miseries were not at an end. Some kind of infection-spreading insects (possibly lice), had been found on board, so on arrival at Aomori harbor the passengers were told they would have to remain on the ship for a week of quarantine. Like the first vessel it was old and rusty, and as they sat in the hold for their meager meals their breath condensed on the rusty iron ceiling, and they had to put up umbrellas to prevent the unpleasant, dirty drippings from falling into their food.

At last the quarantine was completed and they could disembark. They were all herded onto the quayside and very liberally sprayed with DDT, a somewhat dubious welcome to their longed-for homeland.

Chapter Seven

Rock Bottom

ALTHOUGH THERE HAD BEEN NO POSTAL SERVICE between Sakhalin and Japan since the end of the war, the Tamuras had been able to send messages to their relatives in Kominato by friends who had left before them. So, during the week's quarantine Tozaburo, the eldest Tamura brother, had had time to find their names and learn when they would disembark.

There were many relatives and friends to meet the hundreds of passengers, and when they were finally allowed through the barrier, reeking with DDT, it took a while for everyone to get sorted out, especially as some had not seen their relatives for thirty years or more. But at last Tozaburo, with his wife and daughter, spotted Tazaburo.

The customary deep bows were exchanged, the formal greetings and the murmurs of 'It's a long time, isn't it?' Michiko found it a little hard to tell how welcome they really were. She eagerly looked at the three faces and thought at once how like her own mother the daughter, Matsuno, was. Michiko thought she would like the new Ojii-san, too, but she wasn't quite sure about the Obaa-san — somehow there was a rather remote, stern air about her.

The older members of her own family looked around for former landmarks as they slowly followed the crowds up the steps and along the railway bridge which led to the platform from which the train to Kominato would leave. The city had been badly bombed, however, for it was both an important rail terminus and the main port for ships going to and from Hokkaido. Some rebuilding had already begun, but this was very cheap and drab-looking. The Japanese economy was barely beginning the recovery which was later to amaze the world.

Michiko looked around with equal interest, but for her it was the excitement of the new and unknown. She was grateful that the sea and coastline were more friendly-looking than the fierce breakers crashing against her native cliffs. The mountains a few miles away were comfortingly familiar, and the crowds of sad-looking, shabbily-dressed people at the station did not seem very different from those she had become used to recently in Sakhalin.

The train journey to Kominato was crowded, too, but fortunately lasted less than an hour. Michiko's bright eyes eagerly took in everything on their way from the station as she wondered for the hundredth time what their new home would be like. Finally they turned the last corner, and there it was.

She liked what she saw. The house was old, but spacious-looking, and there was a nice yard. Michiko quickly ran her eyes over the members of the family as they lined up to give the official welcome greeting to the house. There was Tozaburo and his wife, their adopted daughter Matsuno with her husband who had also been adopted into the family, and their three children. Michiko noted with regret that one of these was older and the other two younger than herself. Seven in this family and seven in her own; quite a houseful! But at least she wasn't likely to be lonely, she concluded, little dreaming that she would in fact spend some of the loneliest months of her life in this house.

They were shown the big room their family was to live in, and after a simple supper they began to feel a little more relaxed with these nearly unknown relatives. There had been little opportunity for talk on the crowded train, but now they had finished eating and there was a lull in the polite small talk of which the conversation had consisted up till now. Finally Tozaburo asked the question for which his younger brother had been waiting.

'Do you know when Tajiro's wife and family will be arriving?'

'Oh, they are coming then? We haven't had word from them recently. Communication has been very difficult in Karafuto. We tried to send them word when we knew we were coming out, but I don't know if they received it or not.'

'They received their permits soon after you, I learned from someone on the ferry that came before yours. I would think they may be here any day now.'

'Well, that's good! But — where will they go?'

'Where else can they go?' Tozaburo's face was expressionless.

'There are seven of them, you know,' Tazaburo answered a little apprehensively.

'And Yojiro's wife and family are trying to get out, too,' Tozaburo's wife added, with a grim look.

Michiko's grandfather suppressed a little groan. 'Another five! That's 26 in all! How are we going to manage?'

'The harvest is fairly good this year. I think there will be just enough rice for us all. But little else.'

Michiko saw her grandfather suddenly sag as he sat cross-legged at the low table. She knew he must be tired after their terrible journey, and probably reaction was setting in now. 'Perhaps he had hoped to be quiet for a few days while he got his bearings in his childhood home,' she thought.

Actually, Tazaburo had always been closest to his older brother, and it had seemed the natural thing for him to come home and receive a welcome. But their younger brothers had been dead some time and taking in all their families seemed rather much to expect.

'Is there nowhere else — ?' he began.

'Nowhere,' his brother answered flatly. 'And we have an obligation. Yojiro and his wife gave us Matsuno, remember.'

Although the evening was quite warm, Michiko was surprised to see her grandmother suddenly snatch up a bamboo fan from a side table and begin fanning herself rapidly. They hardly needed fans in Karafuto. Tozaburo's wife, too, suddenly began clearing away the supper things. Matsuno gave Umeno a quick, half-smile before following her adopted mother to the kitchen. These two women were soon to have the strange experience of being under the same roof as their natural mothers, from whom they had been separated as children.

Michiko's family had been in Kominato a week and were beginning to feel more or less settled, when a neighbor came with news that Tajiro's family were on the passenger list of the ferry due next day. So they all had to adjust once more, until each found his respective place and established a routine. Everyone except Tozaburo's wife and Michiko went off to the rice fields in the early morning, and were busy there all day. In the evening supper was served in three sittings, and by the time it was all cleared away it was bed time, so they didn't really get in each other's way.

Finally, a month later, Yojiro's family of five arrived, and once again there was the effort to adjust to new circumstances. Gradually the men managed to erect a kind of lean-to building on the side of the house, where the smaller family lived as best they could. In normal circumstances it would have been utterly unthinkable to live in such crowded conditions, but in fact they were among the more fortunate of the Japanese people at that time.

For the past few months, over six million repatriates from Taiwan, Manchuria, Korea, Sakhalin and the Kuriles had been returning to the home islands of Japan. Many found no relatives alive or home standing. Numerous cities and towns had been devastated by bombings, and the only dwellings were shacks hastily thrown together with the debris. People were living in tunnels and air-raid shelters, and even in the open at first, without proper clothing, bedding or sanitation. Many actually died of starvation, or else from tuberculosis which struck down thousands.

Including those who had been in the huge military forces and the war industries supporting them, there were now thirteen million unemployed, and even for those who had work, wages were only a third of what they had been in 1930. Thousands of wounded and crippled soldiers were forced to beg or starve, and often received more compassion from the Occupation forces and other foreigners than from their own people. At first reparations were demanded by all the countries who had suffered from Japanese aggression, but it was soon evident to the Allied Occupation officials that vast stocks of food, clothing and medicines must be brought into the country if the lives of millions of its citizens were to be saved. Probably nowhere in the history of the world had there been a more benevolent occupation, nor a more cooperative subject people, as together they worked for the reconstruction of life in Japan.

The hard-working Tamura clan did their part, as we have seen, by providing shelter for all the relatives in need and also by working their rice fields to the utmost.

Before long school reopened after the summer vacation and Michiko, having been denied a teacher for three years, was looking forward to this with characteristic eagerness. Yet she later said that here her 'real suffering' began.

She was still a stranger to many of the children of the neighborhood, and most had never seen a cripple before. It was still the custom to keep such people hidden away, except for the homeless wounded soldiers who were now allowed to go through the trains to beg from passengers. So, when Michiko first appeared at school, the other children poked endless fun at her, saying the most cruel things. Some of them, too, spoke to her in the strong Aomori dialect which she didn't always understand, and that was very frustrating for her as well.

Her breaking point came when they began to follow her to the toilet, and wouldn't let her shut the door. She tried asking to go in the middle of class, but even then some always managed to follow her. Michiko had the natural embarrassment of a normal teenage girl and at this her spirit really broke for the first time in her life. After two months she absolutely refused to go to school. Her grandparents tried to make her go, the teacher called and tried to persuade her to return, but to no avail. She remained adamant and refused even to discuss the matter.

Possibly Michiko unconsciously felt the hurt more deeply because it was so utterly unexpected, and because it came from her own Japanese people whom those on Karafuto had always spoken of with such respect. For two years her family's one longing had been to escape from Soviet occupation back to their own people where, in fantasy, it seemed that everything would be good again. Yet Michiko had had some real friends among the Russian children and had always been made so welcome at school before. Perhaps, too, the new stirrings of teenage mental and physical development made her more vulnerable. At any rate, for whatever reason Michiko for the first and only time in her life 'gave up'. She saw life as nothing but a dark, utterly disagreeable tunnel stretching endlessly before her, and she no longer had any desire to live.

As winter came and the adults were not quite so busy in the fields, tensions became more frequent in the house; worst of all, the two grandfathers began drinking in the evenings, together and with the sons-in-law of Tajiro and Yojiro. They fermented their own rice wine, so it wasn't a burden on the very frail family finances; but Michiko's grandfather had stopped drinking some years before on account of his heart condition, so now the rest of his family were quite concerned. It was very unpleasant for all the women and children, too, because often the men would grow quarrelsome and abusive, and the women, including those with babies on their backs, would have to walk up and down in the cold outside, waiting until the men had fallen asleep or were too far gone to pick a fight, before they dared venture in to bed. The men were not basically bad and would apologize in the morning for their behavior, but even so they would repeat it again the next night; drinking seemed their only relief from the tedium and hardship of life in those days. It was while drunk, too, that the sons-in-law would start trying to claim a legal share of the farm, and that naturally upset Tozaburo.

Fortunately the women all remained on good terms, perhaps because they were all so closely related, so the situation was not nearly as bad as it might have been with so many women under one roof.

Spring came at last. The adults in the family began staying out in the fields all the hours of daylight, taking cold riceballs along for their lunch. Michiko, left with only the 'house Obaa-san' who still remained rather remote, experienced then the loneliest period of her life. There wasn't even a cat in the house because they couldn't afford to spare food for any animal. One day, however, she remembered the chickens they used to have in Karafuto. If only she could have just one as her special pet and friend!

There was no money to buy one, she knew. But she had learned how a chicken is hatched, so one day when she was alone with her grandmother and mother she decided now was the time to ask.

'Do you think I could have an egg for myself?'

'An egg? Whatever for? You know how difficult it is for us to buy anything extra these days,' scolded her grandmother.

'I'd like to try and hatch one, to have a chicken of my own. I'm so lonely here all day with nothing to do. It would be a friend for me.'

'If only you went to school you wouldn't be lonely. It's your own fault,' Taka grumbled.

'Perhaps the chicken would eventually lay eggs, and that would help us all,' her mother suggested tentatively. Her heart ached for Michiko as she realized what she had gone through at school, and that here there was so little for her to do. Michiko was obviously a liability to the big family circle, too, and that is never a happy position to be in.

Taka looked doubtful, but evidently was persuaded by this logic, for she finally said, 'Well, see if you can get one that has been fertilized next time you go to market.'

When the day came that her mother brought home the egg, Michiko held it in her hands with almost reverent joy. She begged her grandmother to get her a hot-water bottle, then carefully covered the egg with fluffy cotton and placed it snugly against the warmth. Periodically through the day she replaced the warm water, and began to imagine what the chicken would look like, and what she would name it.

On the third day after getting the egg, her mother came into the room, a look of anxiety on her face. She stood beside Michiko for a few minutes, watching her apprehensively as she rearranged the hot-water bottle.

'I'm terribly sorry, Miko-chan,' she said at last. 'There is an unexpected guest coming, and Obaa-san has asked for the egg to make something a little special for him.'

For a long moment Michiko stared at her mother, her face frozen with grief. Then silently she pulled away the cotton and with careful fingers tenderly removed the egg. Still silent, she slowly handed it over to her mother. Guests had to be treated with honor, that was an irrevocable law which she could not argue against. Only after her mother had left the room did Michiko allow the tears to come, as a feeling of utter desolation and loss overwhelmed her. Could life ever be worth living again?

Chapter Eight

New Vistas at the Village Temple

WEEKS PASSED, then months, with no word of Susumu. They didn't know if he was alive or dead. If a neighbor couldn't do it for them, Umeno had to go into Aomori once a week to check if his name was on the list of passengers on the next repatriation ship. Each time it was the same.

'No, there's no news of him yet,' she would say in response to Taka's enquiring look.

Now it was winter again and Tazaburo, who wasn't really fit to work in the fields and was no longer needed there, began to visit their local temple of the Monto, or Jodo Shin (True Pure Land) Buddhist sect.

During the war there had been little time for religion, except for the emphasis on State Shinto worship made compulsory by the military government. Even now, everyone was desperately busy trying to get back on their feet financially, so that most temples had suffered considerably from neglect. Tazaburo became friendly with the priest who was now back in residence in this particular temple, and began to go and help in various ways, largely to find something to do and get out of the house occasionally. Then one morning in early spring he had an idea.

'Miko-chan, how would you like to come with me to the temple?' he asked. 'You could be quite a help there polishing the brasses.'

Michiko eagerly agreed, glad of the prospect of anything to do after the loneliness and monotony of the house. The temple was less than ten minutes walk away, too, so she could manage to get there on her crutches.

It was depressing and a little scarey to find she was to work in the room where the ashes and bones of some of the village dead were stored in urns. And it soon grew tiring to sit there for hours with only her grandfather for company. But there was some satisfaction in making the various candlesticks, vases, incense pots, censors and tongs shine brightly again. They reminded her too of the Russian children who had stolen such utensils from the deserted temples in Mototomari.

At first she asked her grandfather what some of the things were used for and once, while he collected the items to be polished, she peered into the dimly-lit main worship hall. There she saw the huge, gilded altar, and the statue of Amida, so much bigger than their one at home.

'Ojii-san, where did Lord Amida come from originally?' she asked her grandfather as they began their work. Tazaburo turned one of the beautiful vases around in his hands a moment before replying.

'Why, surely you know that by now,' he said a little testily. 'He was a Bodhisattva who made a vow not to accept the supreme Enlightenment of Buddhahood unless he could share his merits with everyone, and help them to Enlightenment.'

'And what happened?'

'Well, he must have accumulated a vast store of merits, and attained Buddhahood. Then he established the Pure Land, our Western Paradise. That's where we shall be reborn in the future, if we have faith in him, you know.'

'Yes, yes.' Michiko had certainly heard that many times. 'I just wondered *when* he lived, and where he came from.'

'I don't believe anybody knows. But that's not important,' Tazaburo added impatiently. 'All we need to do is have faith in him, then we shall go to the Pure Land when we die. Now you finish cleaning these while I see the priest for a few minutes.' He left carrying a bottle of their home-brewed rice wine.

The Jodo Shin School of Buddhism*, to which the Tamura family belonged, had little in common with the original teachings of Buddhism. The ideas from which it came probably arose in India as a result of Christian influence, and the sect was formed by a priest named Shinran in the twelfth century AD, who taught that repeating the phrase 'Adoration to the Lord of boundless light' as an invocation to Amida, and believing in it, ensured salvation and rebirth in the Pure Land. This 'easy way' of Amidaism appealed strongly to the common

---

*For more details on this Sect see Appendix 4.

people, especially with its promise of life after death, and it soon had
the largest following of all Japanese schools of Buddhism.

One of the teachings of the sect was that if a person commits
suicide with the name of Amida on his lips he will be welcomed into
Paradise by 25 Bodhisattvas seated on purple clouds. This encouraged
lovers whose parents would not sanction their marriage to commit
joint suicide in the hope of happiness together there. It also explains
why Michiko had so often been counselled by her grandparents to
take her life if anything happened to them or her parents.

With the Meiji Restoration this sect became a national leader in
the fields of scholarship and social welfare. As a result, many temples
acquired good libraries, and one day Michiko made the thrilling
discovery that in her village temple there was a good collection of
books. This brought a leap of joy to her heart, and when she was told
she could read all she wanted the old sparkle returned to her eyes.

Soon afterwards, her grandfather also made a discovery during an
evening visit to the temple.

'The priest's daughter† has just returned home after taking a
dress-making course,' he announced to the family with an air of
importance. 'This now qualifies her to teach and she will begin a class
in two weeks time. So I asked if Michiko could attend, and she says
she may try,' he finished.

'Well, that's kind of her,' Taka said. 'And it will be a help to the
family if you can at least mend our clothes properly, Michiko. But I
wonder if you will be able to use a sewing machine?'

'Oh, I'm sure I can.' There was a touch of the old enthusiasm now.

'You might even be able to make simple things for us,' her mother
put in, 'there's beginning to be more material in the shops now. But it
seems many people are going in for those western-style skirts, as they
take less material.'

'You will never find me wearing one,' said Taka firmly. 'I don't
know what our country is coming to. The kimono has always been our
national dress.'

No one cared to argue with her and the subject was dropped, but
Michiko waited impatiently for the class to begin.

Her hands, on which she was so dependent, were deft in all they
did, and she soon learned to manage the sewing machine. Then after

---

†In original Buddhist teaching only the celibate can hope to reach Enlightment. But
one of Shinran's innovations had been to marry openly, and this practice continued in
most sects which included the worship of Amida among their tenets.

the class she would go to the library. Although some of the books didn't interest her, she found good novels and biographies, so in spite of having had only four years of school, she managed to continue her education and to learn and practise writing more of the several thousand Chinese characters an educated person needed to know.

The days once more passed quickly and happily for Michiko as she faced these new challenges to both mind and body. In fact she has always remained very grateful to the priest and his daughter for their kindness to her, and for the skills acquired there in the temple which were to become a springboard to as-yet-undreamed-of accomplishments.

Chapter Nine

Susumu Returns

WITH THE COMING OF SPRING Michiko especially enjoyed the quiet of the temple gardens, away from the noise and bustle of the narrow village streets. They formed a little bird sanctuary, too, and soon were gay with flowers as summer finally came to the cold north.

Just as her life seemed really settled into this pleasant routine, Michiko returned home one day to find her sister Miyoko ill with a high fever, and her grandmother looking very apprehensive.

'It seems very like when you were first ill, Miko-chan,' she said.

Next morning Miyoko was no better, so tying her on her back her mother set out for the station, to take her to the big hospital in Aomori. Umeno's heart was tight with anxiety as she tried to shield the child as much as possible from the gaze of the other passengers. At last they arrived in Aomori, and as she walked down the long platform she tried to speak reassuringly to the little girl on her back; but there was no reply.

With growing fear, Umeno tried to hurry faster towards the hospital. Sweat poured down her face from the heat of the sun, and the exertion of carrying such a burden, yet it seemed to her that the fever-ridden body on her back was a little cooler.

There was the hospital at last. Impatiently she went through all the admittance procedures and finally was in the doctor's office. With trembling fingers she untied the knots of the cloth which had supported Miyoko on her back, and gently let her down onto the waiting chair.

One look was sufficient and she did not need to hear the doctor's verdict. Polio had taken the life of her beautiful little Miyoko, and Umeno had to face the death of a third child.

Clumsily she hitched the stiffening body onto her back again, trying to cover as much of it as possible with the carrying cloth, then set off for the return trip to Kominato. What a nightmare journey! Not until she reached the shelter of the house could she allow the tears to flow.

All in the big household were sad at the loss of cheerful little Miyoko. A simple funeral was conducted by Tazaburo's friend, the priest. The family tried to comfort Umeno with the thought that it was better for Miyoko to be dead than to be crippled like Michiko. At least it was one mouth less to feed, for money was still desperately short.

Michiko's mind was a whirl of conflicting questions.

'Why did I stay alive, and Miyoko die so quickly? Wouldn't it have been better if I had died too, instead of being left with these dead legs?'

Yet life had begun to be pleasant again at the temple and she knew she had no desire to die just now.

It was a welcome distraction for Umeno when one day her husband's name finally appeared on the passenger list of the next repatriation ship. Her excitement spread throughout the household as they prepared for his coming. Personally Michiko couldn't honestly feel she had missed her father much, and she supposed it would mean one more to crowd their bedroom. She believed that the sight of her legs really embarrassed or annoyed him, and was thankful that she could at least be out of his sight at the temple much of the day.

Tozaburo, Michiko's grandfather and her mother all went to the Aomori docks to meet Susumu, while the rest stayed expectantly at home, ready to line up and give him the formal greeting.

At last he arrived, looking very tired and older, but otherwise not very different. After the formal bows, during which he hardly seemed to notice Michiko, they all went into the living room, Susumu carrying the one bundle which was all he had been able to bring out of Karafuto.

His eyes travelled quickly over the assembled company, then back again.

'Where is Miyoko-chan?' he asked.

There was silence for a moment. It was Taka who broke it.

'She was very sick a few weeks ago — the same thing Miko-chan had — but unfortunately she didn't recover.'

A stricken expression suffused Susumu's face. *'What?'* he whispered, thunderstruck and upset. After escaping all the dangers on Karafuto and finally reaching his homeland again, it was ironically unexpected to find tragedy awaiting him there. He slumped a little, still sitting in the ceremonial position on the floor; then with an angry look at Michiko he burst out, 'Why couldn't it have been *you*?'

The words stabbed Michiko's heart like a sword-thrust. Why did he have to come back and bring her so much unhappiness? Was there no end to the suffering she was to meet here?

With a weary gesture Susumu pulled the bundle tied in its *furoshiki* in front of him, and slowly undid the four knots. Somehow he had managed to get a gift for the 'house Obaa-san,' for no one can visit in Japan without taking a present. For his parents he had brought a very special kind of hat as a souvenir of Karafuto. Then there were three children's gifts. He gave Ichiro and Shooji theirs, and held the last in his hands.

'This was for Miyoko-chan,' he said brokenly.

The sword in Michiko's heart pierced deeper still, but with a fierce pride she kept the tears back. Her father had planned no gift for her — perhaps he had hoped she was dead already! And he didn't even give her now the one he had brought for her little sister. For a moment life once more seemed no longer worth living. Perhaps after all she should take the poison her grandparents kept reminding her was there...... But then she remembered the books and sewing machine at the temple. She would keep on living, no matter what her father wanted. She'd just *show* them!

The large, crowded household was no doubt a shock to her father after being alone for so long; and being an adopted member of the family and not a real Tamura probably made him conscious of a little inferiority. There is a Japanese saying, 'While you have even a pint of rice bran left, do not allow yourself to become an adopted child'. But at five years of age Susumu had had no choice.

He lost no time looking for work, and since he had a long record of railway service he was soon appointed station master at the little branch line station of Hamango, just outside Kominato. This line had been hastily pushed through to the coast during the war, after Aomori harbor had been destroyed and temporary port facilities had been developed near Kominato. Hamango was little more than a small hamlet of houses and dormitories which had been built for defence personnel in the war but were now available for railway workers.

Susumu came home one evening with a triumphant look on his face.

'I've been granted one of the houses in Hamango,' he told his wife. 'We can move out there at the end of the month.'

Michiko turned cold at this news. Was this to be the end of all her happy days at the temple? She fought to keep back the tears, but then they froze in anger at her father's next words.

'It's only a small place. I don't know what Father and Mother will wish to do in the circumstances, but we'll leave Michiko here.'

So her father wanted to get rid of her for good! Would her grandparents, too, she wondered bitterly.

Fortunately for her, Tazaburo decided he did not want to be banished to Hamango, which was too far from the temple where he now had a strong interest, as well as a lay position of some responsibility. So the final decision was that Michiko and her grandparents would stay in Kominato while her two brothers moved out to Hamango with their parents. So Michiko too was able to continue her pleasant existence at the temple.

Eventually, however, the priest's daughter had so many would-be students that her room at the temple wasn't big enough and a more suitable place had to be found further away. It turned out to be actually closer to Hamango, and as Michiko had almost completed the course she was allowed to move out to live with her parents. Her mother carried her on her back twice a week to the school, before going off herself to help in the rice fields.

Michiko sadly missed the temple library and at first tried to borrow discarded text books from the neighbors. Then one day she saw in the newspaper an advertisement from one of the famous universities in Tokyo, offering correspondence courses for Middle School. She begged so much to be allowed to take this that the family finally consented, and she began working on the course. By now she was 18 and skilled enough to be paid for her work, so she was able to take in sewing to be done at home. What a triumphant day it was when she received her first pay, and knew she need no longer be completely dependent on others!

By this time her grandparents were growing more feeble, and they too decided to move to Hamango, where Michiko was able to care for them to some extent. Before long Tazaburo was too weak to get up, and they placed his mattress facing the godshelf with its image of Amida. He was obviously in much pain, and Taka kept saying, 'Ask the Lord Amida to heal you.' But though he went through his prayer beads many times, counting out the *nembutsu* (invocations), he only grew worse and instead began to repeat, 'I don't want to die, I don't want to die.'

This surprised Michiko. She thought the idea of the Western

Paradise would be very appealing if you were in such pain as Ojii-san obviously was.

Susumu even offered the hat he had brought back as a souvenir of Karafuto to the doctor, as an inducement to give some specially potent medicine to her grandfather; Michiko doesn't remember what was so unusual about the hat but it was apparently not meant for ordinary wear. Perhaps it was one of those that Chinese emperors in earlier days had bestowed on Gilyak and Oroki chiefs, to denote their rank. If so, it would certainly have been valuable. But even this was of no avail.

One morning Tazaburo awoke feeling especially cold and weak, and Michiko and her grandmother knelt on the straw matting on either side of his mattress, massaging his hands in the hope of restoring the circulation. Taka also put his prayer beads over his hands, but he gave a sudden jerk which flung them in the direction of the godshelf.

'There is no Western Paradise!' His cold lips uttered the words in a weak, but clear voice. Then he sank back, lifeless.

His death shocked Michiko in several ways. For the first time she realized that the body wasn't everything, and that mind and body were separate. Until now she had thought so much about her own body and its inadequacies, which kept her from the many things she wanted to do.

'But even though my legs seem dead, as useless as Ojii-san's are now,' she told herself, 'I still have a mind, and hands as alert and active as anyone's. I must be thankful for that, and use them while I can.'

The greatest shock, however, had been to hear her grandfather's words implying there was nothing after death. If this was so, why did all the people come to the house and make such a fuss at the funeral, as if it were a great event? Because Tazaburo had been head of the family, and also a valued official at the local temple, it was a very elaborate funeral indeed. There were many candles, much burning of incense, reading of Sutras and intoning of prayers for the dead. Then the priest took a razor wrapped in white paper and laid it on Tazaburo's head, to indicate he had received the tonsure of a priest. After that came the words, 'Leaving this world of change where true thankfulness and affection never come, pass on to the realm of peace where true love and gratitude ever abide.' This was repeated three times and was followed by an invocation to Amida.

As she listened, Michiko wondered if these thrice-repeated words could undo her grandfather's lack of belief. Finally the priest wrote his posthumous name on a narrow wooden plaque — the longer the name, the bigger the expense, of course. Afterwards the plaque was reverently placed on the godshelf, indicating that his spirit had joined the family ancestors. The candle-burning and chanting continued for the seven days the spirit was supposed to linger around the house.

Why had her grandfather changed his thinking towards the end, Michiko kept wondering. Perhaps it was the result of his closer acquaintance with the priest. By the 1920s few priests, even of the Jodo Shin Sect, believed in either Buddha or Paradise;* these were just regarded as 'convenience devices' to satisfy the common people. Anyone who had studied Buddhist writings knew that 'the doctrine of salvation through faith in Amida was nothing more than a baseless superstition'. Prayers and invocations were not addressed to a real Buddha or Amida, but merely to empty space, or for tranquilizing one's own spirit. Priests carried out these practices because there seemed no other way to get an income for the temples.

After the war, many younger priests and laymen were in a state of despair, and were calling for radical change and a reinterpretation of Amida and the 'Pure Land' in conformity with modern science. So possibly Tazaburo had already heard rumors of these developments in his frequent visits to the temple. Or perhaps it was just that, being an intelligent man himself, the whole procedure had struck him as false when he faced the reality of death.

If, as Michiko now began to suspect, there was no Paradise after death, she certainly had no wish to take the poison her grandfather had always recommended she should have ready when he died. On the contrary, she felt a strong desire to see and enjoy as much of the world as possible.

Often when she was much younger, and had fretted and fussed about wanting to do things the family would not allow, her mother had consoled her by saying, 'Wait until Ojii-san dies, or until you are twenty and of legal age. Then you can do what you want.'

Now Ojii-san was dead, and Michiko suddenly remembered with a ripple of excitement that in a few weeks she would be twenty. What was the future going to hold for her — or, rather, what could *she* now *make* it hold?

*Taisei Michihata, *From Buddha to Christ*. Michihata himself had a growing sense of hypocrisy as he chanted Sutras and prayers before gilded altars and images.

Chapter Ten

A New Life For Michiko

SOON AFTER HER GRANDFATHER'S DEATH, Michiko learned from the newspaper that a commercial night school was to open in Aomori city. She had finished the Middle School course, and now set her heart on attending this. She waited until Tazaburo had been dead for 49 days, after which period his spirit was certain to have left the house, according to Buddhist teaching; then the following evening she made her request to the family. The result was predictable.

'Impossible,' said her father instantly. 'There are no trains to get you there and back in the evening.'

'And you couldn't live there by yourself. Besides, we need you at home,' her grandmother added firmly.

'It would be very hard work, and with men and women there — they might tease, or even ostracize you,' murmured her mother. 'And I'm sure the teachers wouldn't want to be bothered with you.'

Undaunted, Michiko tried again the next night to persuade them, and the next, and the next. The result was always the same and eventually her father ordered her not to mention it again. The rest of the family had talked it over and were convinced it would be dangerous for her to be out at night in the city. Also, they couldn't believe anyone would ever hire her for an office job, even if she passed the secretarial course. Therefore it would all be a waste of money, as well as probably leaving Michiko more dissatisfied and frustrated than ever. So, in spite of all her pleadings, they remained adamant.

Michiko's heart was set on going to the city, however. On further investigation she learned there were two big sewing schools in Aomori which not only offered the basics she had already, but design and teacher training as well. Her spirits lifted at the news. The family knew she had already been able to learn sewing and get some income from it, so they couldn't say it would all be wasted. After a few more nights of argument, with her mother now on her side, it was finally agreed she might at least write to the two schools.

The first she applied to had over 250 students and a very high reputation. Their reply stated they had never had a crippled student, and didn't think they could admit her. The second, smaller school sent a sympathetic letter saying they thought a girl in her condition needed a trade more than anyone, and that if she was able to find her own room to live in they would accept her as a student.

Instead of joyfully accepting this offer, as her family expected, Michiko spent three days thinking hard. She wanted with her entire being — mind, body and spirit — to go to the best school! She felt she had experienced so much suffering in life already that nothing could ever be worse. Whatever conditions she might face, she wanted to prove that she could stick it out.

So she wrote to the first school again, and waited eagerly each day for the mailman to bring their reply. At last it came, and she tore open the envelope her mother handed to her. They now rather grudgingly agreed that she could go for a year's trial, but could not be registered as a regular student.

Well, she would show them! Her family tried to talk her into settling for the smaller school, but she wouldn't listen. She herself wondered sometimes why she was so stubborn, as her family repeatedly called her! Now a thought half formulated itself in her mind — this seemed to be something she couldn't help, part of her very nature. 'I must have been "dug out of rock",' she mused, remembering those great cliffs around the coast of her native Mototomari, against which the waves broke relentlessly but ineffectively. Whatever might happen to her personally, however difficult the work or living conditions in Aomori might prove to be, she felt a compelling urge to go there. She would never give in. She would *make* them accept her!

So her mother went into the city and found a small room for her to rent near the sewing school; then she and Ichiro went with Michiko to carry her few possessions. They were a little fearful when the time came to leave her, and Umeno gave many last-minute instructions on how to take care of herself. Then they were gone.

At last, for the very first time in her life, Michiko was alone! A slight twinge of fear eroded the excitement she felt, but her sweet mouth set in a determined line and her capable hands grasped her crutches more firmly as she went off to the sewing school.

Once Michiko was in front of a sewing machine it was obvious to all that she knew what she was doing. She enjoyed the classes, too, and soon mastered new techniques of sewing and later designing. When she had completed the prescribed work each day, she could also do other sewing for pay.

The time passed quickly and happily, with none of the problems her family had envisaged. Michiko not only enjoyed the work, but also the companionship of so many other girls around her own age. At the end there was a little ceremony at which certificates were awarded to those who had completed the year's work and, to Michiko's surprise, the school director publicly apologized for not accepting her as a regular student and awarded her a special honors certificate. She also invited her to complete the remaining years of instruction.

Once again however Michiko surprised everyone, this time by asking for a year off. Her family and the sewing school officials thought she was overstrained and needed a rest, but this was not the case. Michiko, having proved that she could live on her own, now had other ambitions. She was still thirsting for a high school education, and thought if she spent some time at home she could eventually persuade her family to let her return to the city and attend night school.

In spite of all she could say, however, they absolutely refused to help in any way. There was too much involved in such a course, they said, both in regard to the variety of subjects needed after she had been away from school for so long, and also the fact that it was a night school. They were also still sure it could never lead to a job for anyone in her condition.

With no one to assist in moving her things, Michiko was helpless, nor did she have enough money to support herself for the years that the course would take. Inwardly consumed with frustration, she had to remain at home that year, doing sewing for those who needed it in the village. She eventually decided to return to the sewing school and complete the remainder of the course which would qualify her to become a sewing teacher, and the family finally agreed to this.

Back in Aomori she was interested to find another crippled girl, named Somma San, had been admitted to the sewing school. Though not so handicapped as Michiko, her condition involved chronic pain, yet she usually remained cheerful.

Michiko also noticed that some of the more recent students were different from those she had known before. They tended to be older, and a number were zealous members of some of the so-called New Religions which had been proliferating in the dark and insecure days of post-war Japan. By 1963 these claimed to have eighteen million adherents. Actually most of the 'New Religions' were simply popularized versions of Shinto and Buddhism, plus a mixture of Christian terminology and teachings, presented in a fresh and striking way with new rites, new buildings and new methods of gaining followers. The reason for their success was no doubt the moral and economic chaos after Japan's defeat in the war, and the consequent blow to national self-confidence and pride.

Common to most of these religions is a strong leader, and a headquarters or 'Mecca' in one of the many famous beauty spots in Japan. They are easy to enter and follow, they are optimistic, and promise to establish the Kingdom of God on earth here and now. Their most frequent claims are the prevention of sickness, healing by faith, and material prosperity. Once having gained adherents they hold them by threats of punishment by the ancestors for various omissions or for defection.

Seeing Michiko with her two useless legs, these women envisaged a promising convert. 'Sickness, poverty, unhappiness will become things of the past, and a happy life with the fulfilment of every human need lies ahead if you will join us,' recited one.

'Come and see the kingdom of God!' explained another. 'There is no worry, sickness, agony or suffering in God's land. God's kingdom is nowhere remote, it sprouts in your heart and grows within ourselves.'

Michiko's old acquaintance, the Seicho no Ie, which had helped with the skilful massage of her hands away back in Karafuto, also had some followers there. 'We wish to overcome diseases and all other miseries of mankind by a true conception of man's life, by a true way of living, and by a true method of education,' was their claim, 'and we want to devote ourselves to establish on earth the Heaven of Mutual Love and Assistance.'

While some could not express so fully the tenets of their faith, the girls each invited Michiko to attend their particular meetings, promising either that she would soon get rich or that her legs would be healed.

These sounded very inviting prospects, yet strangely they held little appeal to Michiko. Her family had been well off once, but they hadn't seemed particularly happy then; and now it was all lost. With poverty and suffering still prevalent since the war, she didn't see much evidence of many having become rich, either. As for healing, Michiko still had vivid and painful memories of all her grandmother's efforts to find a cure for her as a child, and she wanted no repetition of them.

Why couldn't people accept her as she was, useless legs and all? She was a *person,* not just a crippled curiosity. How many times she had felt frustrated in the face of this prevalent attitude!

She still remembered her disillusionment at her grandfather's death, too, and now it was even more distracting to have all these new ideas thrust at her. Why did there have to be so many religions, and why did their followers keep pestering her so much? If only she could just settle on one, perhaps the others would stop bothering her! But she couldn't have confidence in Amida any more. 'Surely there must be only one true religion,' she began to think, 'but how am I ever to know which is the right one?'

It wasn't long before Michiko noted, with some surprise, that the other students didn't seem to bother Somma San, the other lame girl. Curious about this, she decided to invite her round to her room on Sunday, usually a holiday at the sewing school, to see if she could discover what Somma San had said to make the other girls stop urging her to join them.

'Somma San,' she began, when they had finished work that day, 'Are you free this Sunday morning? I'd like to invite you over to my room.'

Somma San looked rather startled at this unusual invitation from someone she hardly knew.

'I'm sorry,' she said hesitantly, 'I'm never free on Sunday mornings.'

It was Michiko's turn to be surprised, but she was too polite to ask why. Instead she decided to broach the subject which was filling her mind these days.

'It's not like it was the first year I was here,' she said in a low voice so that she couldn't be overheard. 'All these followers of the New Religions weren't here before, and they keep on pestering me to go with them and get healed. But I notice they don't seem to bother you. Why is it?'

Somma San smiled. 'They did at first. But then I started going to the Christian church, so they stopped.'

'Christian church? What's that?'

'It's the great religion of the Westerners, but it's really for everybody, I've discovered. And there's a man there much more handicapped than either of us.' Remembering Michiko's resentment against the other girls, Somma San decided not to say any more.

'Is it good? Do you really like it?'

'Yes, I do. As a matter of fact, I have become a Christian myself.'

There was such a peaceful expression on Somma San's face, in spite of the pain in her foot, that Michiko, although shocked at what she had just heard, couldn't help feeling strangely impressed.

'Do you think — would it be possible for me to go with you, to see what it's like?' Michiko could hardly believe she had said the words, but in spite of a spasm of fear she determined not to withdraw them.

Somma San looked dubious, however. 'It's the other side of the school from where you live,' she said finally. 'I'm afraid it will be too far for you on crutches. But I'll ask at the church, and see what they suggest.'

The following Monday she came up to Michiko, a smile on her face.

'There's a foreigner at the church, a Mr Fisher, and he says he will come next Sunday and take you to the church on the back of his bicycle.'

Michiko really felt embarrassed on hearing this and almost wished she had never asked to go. It was a long time since she had been near any foreigners — not since the Russians in Karafuto. What would this man be like?

When Mr Fisher appeared on Sunday morning he very soon put her at ease. He was a grey-haired Canadian who had spent many years as a missionary in China. When the Communists turned out the foreigners there and the China Inland Mission decided to begin work in other Asian countries under the new name of Overseas Missionary Fellowship, he had volunteered to come to Japan. This had meant learning another difficult language when not far from retirement, but nothing daunted, Hubert and Mary Fisher had done their best in language school and were now planning to pioneer new work in Aomori prefecture, far from the comparative comforts of Tokyo.

The work in Aomori City had been begun by missionaries of The Evangelical Alliance Mission (TEAM), who had now gone on furlough, leaving a group of believers who were meeting on Sundays in a rented kindergarten room. The Fishers had visited every house in its area, offering tracts and an invitation to the meetings. When Hubert had arrived at the Sewing School he had spoken briefly to the girls about Christ and invited them to the service, but Somma San was the only one who had had the courage to go. She had soon come to a saving faith in Christ, and the change was showing on her face.

On entering the meeting room Michiko was relieved to find that because it was a kindergarten everyone had to sit on the tiny chairs in contorted positions, and so her own legs would not be so conspicuous. She immediately noticed the other cripple there, a Mr Mitsuhashi, who was indeed much more handicapped than herself, yet had such a smiling face. He was a teacher at the OMF language school and it was he, in fact, who had led Somma San to Christ.

Everyone greeted Michiko in a friendly, accepting way. When the service started she was amazed how different it was from anything she had experienced before. The opening songs were so cheerful, and everyone joined in, singing as if they really meant the words. Then came a prayer, so different from any of the Buddhist rituals she had heard. The thing she found most moving — in fact the only words which had any meaning and stuck in her mind that first Sunday — was the phrase 'Our Heavenly Father'. How beautiful it sounded, and so different from her own father, she thought, who seemed so cold toward her that sometimes she still doubted if she was really his child. (Actually they were very much alike in some ways, as one day she was to discover.)

She felt a strong desire to continue going to these meetings. At first the many new words were just a strange jumble and it was the friendly atmosphere which she liked. But soon some words began to make sense. The first sermon she understood was on the text, 'I am the way, the truth and the life.' The conviction then pierced her mind that this was THE way, that there was only one, as she had previously sensed there should be. Contrary to many New Religions, which taught one faith was as good as another and you could take bits from each to suit yourself, she now came to the stark realization that there was only *one* — the teaching of Jesus Christ.

Gradually she learned that, unlike Amida, He was a real, historical person, born in a land called Israel nearly 2,000 years ago, and that western people actually reckoned their calendar by the date of His birth. But not only was He a man in history, He was also the eternal Son of this Heavenly Father the Christians prayed to, and He had come to this world to give His life as a sacrifice for the sin of all people.

From then on all the talk about sin which she had often heard before but hadn't understood, began to make sense. She knew that sin was real in her own life, and more and more came to light as she heard the Bible explained. The biggest sin of all was her hatred of her father, she knew, and this was very hard to give up and repent of. But at last she came to the place where she was willing for this, and finally assurance came that she really had forgiveness because of what Christ had done for her on the cross.

Michiko was 22 years old then, and Hubert Fisher wrote about her to his prayer supporters, 'Miss Tamura ..... continued coming, until one day I could see by her radiant face that Christ was dwelling in her heart by faith.'

Michiko now knew beyond any shadow of doubt that what she was hearing was THE TRUTH, and that only Christ was THE WAY; that now through Him she had a completely new kind of life, and above all a Heavenly Father who loved and accepted her just as she was.

Chapter Eleven

Camp and its Far-reaching Consequences

THE WEEKS SPED BY for Michiko after this great new joy had entered her life. Too soon, it seemed, the year's course would end and it would be time to return to Hamango for the August holiday. At this time all Japanese families try to get together for the traditional Buddhist festival called Obon, when 'the lid of hell is opened'. This releases the spirits of the ancestors and they are welcomed home from the graves for three days. Afterwards they are escorted back with lanterns and colorful ceremonies, varying according to local custom.

Michiko hadn't yet dared to tell any of her family that she was now a Christian, or even that she attended the meetings, and she knew she would miss these terribly back in Hamango.

Then one Sunday she heard some exciting news. Anton and Bernice Netland of TEAM had come to Aomori Ken with the plan of developing a camp site — a quiet place where Christians could go for more intensive instruction and fellowship. This was especially desirable at Obon and New Year when it was hard not to get involved in idolatrous practices at home. There would also be camps to interest non-Christians, for TEAM and other missions had already proved that to bring people away from all the normal pressures of life was a most promising means of evangelism.

Michiko couldn't envisage all this, of course, but it did sound attractive to be able to be with Christians for a whole day or more, and the wonderful thing was that the camp was just outside Kominato!

It had been a real answer to the Netlands' prayers. When they had come from language school two years before, it hadn't been easy to know how to go about finding a place. But one evening a teacher and his wife, who were attending the Aomori church, appeared at their door. A relative of theirs had some property for sale, they said; would the Netlands be interested in seeing it?

So they and Kamata Sensei, the young man who had recently been called to pastor the Aomori church, went to look and found a rather derelict former teahouse, right on the shore of a sheltered shallow bay, just a short distance around the coast from Kominato and in fact within two kilometers of Hamango. With some fixing up and an increase in the washroom facilities, they decided, this could be made adequate to house around fifty people. There was also room at the side to put up an overflow tent, if necessary.

Upstairs were three large rooms with *tatami* flooring, and sliding door partitions which could be removed to produce a women's dormitory. On the ground floor was a similar but rather bigger area which must serve in turn as dining room, auditorium and men's dormitory. To one side of this was the kitchen, and a small room for the speaker. On the ocean side were sliding doors the length of the rooms, with an attractive view of the bay and its small pine-covered islands. The beauty of the location partly compensated for the primitiveness and dilapidation of the simple board structure.

With much prayer and hard work the property had been obtained, remodelled and made ready for the first camp the previous August, 1956. This year's featured speaker was to be Akira Hatori, a man destined to become one of Japan's foremost evangelists. He had recently returned from study in the United States in preparation for a Christian radio ministry, still a barely-tried novelty in which it was hard to interest the average Japanese pastor. Hatori had just begun work as Radio Pastor for the Pacific Broadcasting Association, an organization formed by several Missions to produce Christian radio programs in Japan.

When Michiko had been home for a few days, she mentioned she wished to visit a friend at a Christian camp at the beach.

'But we belong to the Jodo Shin Shu!' exclaimed her grandmother in horror. 'That Yaso religion is evil! You could have been executed for attending such a meeting once.'

'But that was nearly a hundred years ago, Obaa-san! And there's certainly nothing bad about my friend, she's a very kind and helpful person.'

'But what will the priest and neighbors say?' Taka persisted.

'No one will see, it's away outside the village. Don't you remember that old teahouse? Several people I know in the city are going, as well as my friend from the Sewing School. I can't come to any harm.'

Michiko's father wasn't home, and her grandmother was getting old and too tired to argue with her. 'We shouldn't give her any food if she attends these meetings,' she muttered to Umeno.

'Perhaps there's no harm in just a day at the sea,' Michiko was amazed to hear her mother say. 'People are beginning to think it's good for the health. But just don't listen to any teaching there, Michiko.'

Later she added to Taka, 'She'll never get all that way by herself. It's too far. But it's best not to argue, and let her find out for herself.'

So Michiko prayed frequently that it would not rain and early next morning, under dry skies, she painfully made her way on crutches over the rough paths from the hills down to the camp. Her arms ached terribly, but with frequent rests she managed to complete the two kilometer journey.

In the first session Akira Hatori spoke about Christians being the sons and daughters of God by grace, showing what a wonderful privilege that was. This was a truth Michiko had already begun to experience, and her heart warmed to the speaker as he explained so clearly all that was involved. After a happy tea break enjoying the fellowship of so many other Christians, Hatori spoke later in the morning on God having a purpose planned for each individual Christian, and that each one was designed to be a channel of blessing to reach other people for God.

Michiko's eyes were suddenly opened to a world of service she had never dreamed of. As the message developed she had the growing conviction God could use even a crippled person like herself to reach others for His glory. The choice was hers, whether to make herself available to Him or not.

Hatori did not minimize the difficulties. He himself had found Christ largely through the example of a friend in high school. During the war, when the staff of every school included a military officer, the boys had one day been on parade when the officer suddenly demanded to know if there was anyone there who believed in the Christian religion. Only one boy had the courage to confess that he did, and was badly treated in consequence; but his action made Akira determine to know more about this Christianity which evidently meant so much to his friend. Soon he too accepted Christ as his own Savior and Lord through the help of a woman missionary from England.

As he ended, the speaker asked those who wished to give themselves to become a channel of blessing for God, to come forward. Michiko's choice had already been made and eagerly she seized her crutches and made her way to the front with the others. There Akira

Hatori prayed with them, committing each to God for whatever He had planned for them.

The church leaders could be forgiven if they thought that little could be accomplished by this badly handicapped girl. But the natural question was immediately asked, had she been baptized? And the answer was no. Mr Fisher had moved to other work soon after Michiko became a Christian, and the Japanese pastor had only recently come. As the church still met in the kindergarten, the leaders probably thought it would be impossible for someone so crippled to travel far to be baptized; or perhaps she had not yet had the opportunity to tell of her faith.

Now the ocean was right in front of them, and on hearing her testimony Anton Netland and the pastor suggested she should be baptized later that very afternoon! Michiko was in a quandary. She knew her family would object violently if she told them. The average Japanese thought of baptism, rather than the decision of the heart or attendance at services, as the actual step of becoming a Christian.

What was she to do? She would also need a change of clothes, yet if she appeared at home to get them the family would immediately ask questions. And in any case it would be a terrible strain physically, if not impossible, for her to do the double journey.

It didn't occur to Michiko to ask to borrow any clothes; instead she prayed that her Heavenly Father would undertake for this most important step in her life. Then she set out for home.

She had only gone a little way up the hill when to her great joy and amazement she saw a familiar figure coming down. It was her little brother, Shooji, now seven years old.

'Shooji-chan,' she called eagerly, 'you're just the very person I wanted to see!' She leaned heavily on her crutches to get her breath after the difficult ascent.

'What d'you want?' he asked, a little suspiciously.

'I find I need a change of clothes. I want to stay the night with my friends there by the sea. If I go home, I know they will try to keep me there. So Shooji,' Michiko finished, putting on her most winning smile, 'would you please go, and when no one is looking, get some clean underwear and my old cotton kimono? Here's a *furoshiki* to put them in,' and she held out one of the patterned silk or cotton squares the Japanese use for carrying things.

Shooji hesitated a moment. He had no desire to return home just yet.

'*Please,* Shooji, it's most important, and look, I'll buy you a big candy bar if you'll just help me now.'

Shooji really loved Michiko, and the stories she told him, so he finally took the *furoshiki*.

'All right,' he said reluctantly, 'but how am I to do it if Obaa-san is in the room?'

'You can wait until she eats lunch, if necessary, but I must have the things soon after that. I'll wait for a while, and if you can't come back at once then ask for me at the big old teahouse down there,' and Michiko pointed to the beach area.

As soon as he was gone, Michiko sank down on a tree trunk beside the path and closed her eyes to thank her Heavenly Father for this wonderful provision for her need, and to pray for the success of Shooji's mission.

In well under an hour he was back, his eyes bright with excitement.

'I did it!' he exclaimed. 'Obaa-san was just out of the room a few minutes, but didn't see me go in at all. Here they are!' He held out the *furoshiki* to his sister. 'And don't forget the candy!'

'No, I won't! As soon as I get back you shall have it. Thank you *so* much, Shooji-chan. And tell mother I'll spend the night here, and not to worry.'

Michiko knotted the *furoshiki* onto the lower bar of one of her crutches, then started her return journey, refreshed in body and joyful in heart.

She found a feeling of excitement at the camp as everyone looked forward to the coming baptism, the outward sign that those who took part had truly begun a new life in Christ. Cleansed from the sin of their past through faith in His death for them, they now wanted publicly to own Him as Savior and Lord.

The water was very shallow beside the camp and would entail much wading to get where it would be deep enough for immersion. This would be a problem for Michiko, so Anton Netland and Pastor Kamata decided to take her along a spit of land which led to a picturesque bridge and little island further out in the bay. From there they could conduct the baptism more easily. All those attending the conference went along, and even a few local people came to see what was going on. For her family's sake, Michiko was thankful she knew none of them.

Since she had never been able to try swimming, it could have been a frightening prospect for Michiko to disappear under the waters of the bay, but she had decided with all her heart to follow Christ, and if this was part of it then she would meet it with her characteristic courage.

The time at the conference seemed like a foretaste of heaven, and at the end Michiko was sorry to have to say goodbye to those who had gathered there. Some were already known to her at the Aomori church, while others had come from OMF centers in other cities and it was interesting to learn how each had become a Christian. She dreaded the return to her own home where she knew the atmosphere would be so different.

Back at the sewing school for her final year, she resumed fellowship at the church, and the conviction gradually grew that she must somehow tell her family of this wonderful new life found in Christ. She felt certain of their strong opposition, so the way must be prepared with much prayer, but she was growing daily more confident in the power of her new Heavenly Father.

At last a plan came to her, to be carried out when she returned home for New Year celebrations, the most important event of the year for most Asians.

*   *   *

The final preparations were completed. The house was shining from its extra cleaning, torn paper on inner doors and closets had been replaced, and the New Year decorations of evergreens put in their appropriate position. But in spite of the familiar preparations the day had brought a great surprise for the Tamura family.

A stranger had appeared at the door with the astounding news that he was Susumu's elder brother! Susumu was not aware of ever having set eyes on him, for he had only been two years old when his father had committed suicide following a business failure, and the family had been broken up. This new uncle stayed all day filling them in on some of the family history since that time, and was eventually invited to stay the night.

This was going to make Michiko's plan much harder to carry out, and she prayed desperately for the needed courage, and for a successful outcome.

After the specially late supper of noodles the family were seated around the heater, waiting for the magic moment when the temple bell would peal forth, announcing that a fresh year was born and everything could make a new beginning. Susumu was busy refilling wine glasses, for drinking plenty of rice wine was one of the best ways to keep warm in the cold winter, and certainly on New Year's Eve all including the children were expected to enhance their happiness that way.

Michiko quietly pulled out her little Bible and began to read, but no one seemed to notice, or at least to make any remark. She thankfully read a few words of encouragement, and sent up a silent prayer.

Boom! Suddenly the stillness of the icy winter outside was shattered by the first stroke of the great temple bell over in Kominato. Two ... three ... four ... they all sat up straighter, intent on counting. ... Ninety-nine ... a hundred ... a hundred and seven, a hundred and eight!

Everyone started exchanging congratulations and wishing each other a prosperous New Year, and Michiko's father poured more drinks.

Now, Michiko thought to herself, and took a deep breath.

'Father,' she began earnestly, 'there's something I must say to you. For a long time I have had very bitter thoughts against you for the way you have often treated me.....' She could see him getting angry and realized she was being too negative. 'I do want to apologize for the things I've said and the hard feelings. Please forgive me. I have been very self-centered and can see now how wrong I have been.'

She paused for breath, and the family stared at her in astonishment.

'The reason I'm saying this — in fact the reason I've come to realize how wrong I've been — is because I've become a Christian. Without telling you, I was baptized into the Christian church last summer.'

Michiko noticed a strange expression on her mother's face, but Taka's unmistakably changed from amazement to anger and fright.

'The Bible, God's word,' she hurriedly continued, holding up the copy in her hand, 'tells us that we should confess our sins and be reconciled both to our families and fellow men. That's why I have told you this, and hope you can forgive me. Please! I want us all to have the happiest possible New Year.'

Her heart was in her mouth as she bowed deeply and then turned her bright eyes on them all. It was obvious they were moved. She had certainly been guided to the right moment for her announcement, when they were mellowed by New Year spirit and nostalgia. Yet the family couldn't help being impressed with the change in the former stubborn, self-centered Michiko — as they had often thought her — which could cause her to apologize as she had just done.

For a moment longer no one said a word, then they all began

asking questions at once. 'What are Christians?' 'What kind of a God is this?' 'Where did you get that book?'

So the way was open for Michiko to begin explaining some of the truths which meant so much to her now.

'Jesus died for my sins and rose from the dead,' she told her family. 'I have received His salvation and now He is with me. No matter what happens, in times of perplexity, trouble, suffering, He is always with me, and will help solve the problems and lead me. This is His promise. I believe in this God. I have entered this faith. If at all possible I would like my father to enter it,' she finally pleaded. 'How about it?'

It was all completely new to them and perhaps the wine made it hard for them to think clearly at that point. But Michiko's father and uncle discussed it for a few minutes and finally her father said, 'Well, our country's Constitution guarantees freedom of religion now, and you are of age. For a person like *you*,' with a meaningful glance at her legs, 'perhaps it's all right to follow this Jesus.'

Taka still looked upset. 'I don't see how you can go against all our family has believed, and everyone in this area. I knew no good would come of your going into the city! We certainly would never be able to arrange a marriage for you with those strange beliefs. But' — she sighed heavily — 'It's impossible for you to get married anyway. Isn't it time we slept now?'

In the morning she was still grumbling to Umeno in the kitchen. 'It's downright stupid and selfish of Miko-chan to do what she told us. What will the neighbors think?'

'Yes,' Umeno agreed with a troubled look. 'It's all very well for the government to say these things, but no one up here seems to take any notice and it's here we have to live.'

'We must just be firm and stop giving her any food. That has always brought people to their senses in the past,' Taka continued angrily.

'But she's not often home, and has some money of her own, remember.'

'She'll have to come home after she finishes this course. No one in the city will employ a cripple, and once she's back here she'll have no way of continuing this evil religion. Nobody will ever let it enter *here*, we can be certain of that.'

Chapter Twelve

A Bridgehead in Hamango

WHEN THE NEW YEAR HOLIDAY WAS OVER, Michiko's mother went back with her to Aomori, to carry her things and help her get settled again. As the next day was Sunday, Michiko begged her mother to attend church with her.

'Me? Go to a Christian church? Impossible!' Umeno looked terrified at the very thought.

'There's no reason at all why you shouldn't. You'll enjoy it, I'm sure. Just come this once, to see what it's like. *Please,* Mother.'

Finally Umeno reluctantly agreed and with obvious misgivings went along to the kindergarten, looking ready to run at the first hint of anything strange or evil. But she stayed to the end.

'What a contrast — the daughter radiantly happy, and the mother looking so worried and suspicious,' Hubert Fisher remarked to his wife. Both happened to be visiting there that day.

'Yes, but she really seems to care for Michiko,' Mary answered. 'We must pray that she too will soon be rejoicing in Christ. Won't Michiko be happy then!'

As the weeks passed and the end of Michiko's course drew near, the director of the sewing school called her aside one day.

'We've had a request from one of the big stores in the city,' she told her, 'asking us to recommend someone to work full time for them on their various sewing needs. I don't know what your plans are for the future, but I believe you would be able to handle this work quite easily.'

Michiko was overjoyed. She had no plans at all as yet, and this' would be a wonderful provision which would enable her to stay in the city and continue attending the church. Without waiting to consult her family, she eagerly accepted the job.

She soon found she enjoyed the work, and also her new independence. How wonderful it was to receive her pay, knowing she had earned it, and was not receiving charity or being an obvious burden on her family.

By now she felt really accepted at the church, and was making friends among the other young people there. They were all encouraged to go out on the streets with other Christians and witness in the evenings. Michiko could not go far on her crutches, but she felt one thing she could do sometimes was to invite some of the young people from non-Christian homes to have supper at her place beforehand. The food was simple enough, for Michiko's income was not large and she had been at work all day herself, but her visitors enjoyed it, and they enjoyed too the warm fellowship with other Christians which was so different from usual Japanese custom. Then, after prayer together, they would venture out to witness to their recently-found Savior.

The more Michiko learned of the Christian faith and the need to share it with others, however, the more she began to feel a new pressure, an increasing burden for the salvation of her own family. How was she to tell them more about Christ so they too would want to believe in Him? As she constantly thought about this problem, the obvious answer began to impress itself on her.

'What's the matter?' asked Somma San one evening as she and Michiko were having supper together. 'You don't seem as cheerful as usual. Don't you feel well?'

'Oh, I'm sorry! No, it isn't that. It's — well, I'm beginning to wonder if God wants me to go back home to live, so I can witness to my family.'

'I see. That's always difficult, isn't it. Are there any other Christians in your village yet?'

'Not one. There's the camp nearby, but of course that's only for short periods in the holidays. I hope I'll still be able to go there. But I'm so happy here, I can't bear the thought of leaving and not having the church to go to regularly.'

Not only would Michiko miss the church, but she would lose her wonderful independence as well. Humanly speaking she recoiled from the very thought. But she had a new Master now, and after counting the cost for a few more days she sat down resolutely to write a letter to her parents.

'Here's a letter from Michiko,' Umeno Tamura announced a little hesitantly to her mother and husband one morning.

'Well, what does she say, is she all right?' demanded Susumu.

His wife opened it and carefully studied it for a moment.

'She doesn't mention that, she just asks if she may come home again to live for a while.'

'I knew that work would be too much for her!' her father muttered angrily. 'She should have consulted us before taking on a full-time job like that. But she is always so obstinate!'

'Probably the store wouldn't keep her because she's a cripple. I knew she'd never be able to keep a job,' Taka added.

'She's in a workroom at the back, or does things at home — she doesn't see many of the customers. So I don't think it can be that,' Umeno said gently. 'She has certainly done well so far, much better than we ever expected. She just says she would like to be with us at home again, and she thinks she can earn enough to keep herself by teaching sewing.'

'Who'd be willing to learn from a cripple? And where would she do it? There's no room here.'

'It would probably only be a couple of hours or half days, and it could be when you are working. Then later, perhaps she could rent a room,' Umeno suggested diplomatically. 'Ichiro will soon be leaving for high school in Aomori, so we'll have a little more room and we could use the extra money.'

'Write and tell her to come,' said Taka firmly, before Susumu could reply. 'She's obstinate all right, but there is a bit of improvement since she went away, I must say. Besides, she'll probably forget all this Christian nonsense once she's back home.'

So a few weeks later Michiko arrived back, and soon had some students from among the women of the neighborhood. Many who had grown up during the war years had had no opportunity to learn dressmaking before marriage, as was the usual custom. But now they were getting on their feet again financially, and more materials were available again in the stores, so they were glad to take advantage of this opportunity.

Michiko proved a good and patient teacher, and always seemed to have a smile and an optimistic, victorious spirit which the women found hard to understand in view of her badly-crippled body.

'How can you always be so cheerful?' one of the bolder ones asked. 'We just can't understand it, you being as you are,' she added meaningfully. 'We have never known anyone quite like you!'

So Michiko gladly told them.

'It's just since I've become a Christian. The God of the Christians is a loving heavenly Father, and His Son Jesus Christ came to give His life to save us from our sins. He puts joy in our hearts, and gives us assurance of eternal life.'

The women edged away then, afraid to hear more, but a tiny seed had found a lodging place in their hearts and minds.

Some of Michiko's students had children, and soon she had the idea of starting a meeting for them. Although she had heard about Sunday schools, she had never seen one in action, but that didn't deter her from trying her hand. She had a natural love for children, and they were soon drawn by her smiling face. She taught them Christian songs, and what she herself was reading in the Bible.

After a time some older girls started coming, and a few really believed. Michiko began to meet regularly with them for prayer at 5 a.m. before the day's activities started, and the group saw some unmistakable answers to their prayers. The behavior of many of the children changed for the better, too, and the mothers began to ask what Michiko was teaching them. Finally some of the women enquired if there couldn't be meetings for them too!

Michiko occasionally managed to go into Aomori to attend church, in spite of strong opposition from her family. So the next time she went she asked TEAM missionaries Allen Fadel and Delbert Kuehl if it would be possible to have some special meetings in Hamango. They promised to keep a week free in April, when the worst of the winter would be over.

By this time some of the railway workers had been transferred to Aomori where better housing was now available, and one of the barracks buildings, which had been a men's dormitory, was standing empty. So Michiko got permission to use it for five evenings of meetings. Hastily erected with shoddy materials during the war, it was in bad disrepair with broken windows. Naturally the electricity had been cut off, and Michiko had to beg the nearest neighbor to allow a wire to be strung from his house, so that they might have a light. Some floor braces were broken too, so the *tatami* mats rested at all angles, but this all helped to give an informal atmosphere to the meetings!

Michiko did all she could to get the old barracks patched up, and prayed earnestly that God would bring the people along. There was to be a children's meeting in the early evening, taught by one of the Japanese Christians from Aomori, and she was pretty sure the children would come; but who would have the courage to come to the subsequent adult meeting?

To her surprise and delight about twenty adults came, including her mother, and, most amazing of all, even her father put in an appearance on the nights he was not working. The railway still had the unpleasant practice of requiring 24 hours on duty, and 24 off.

The two missionaries were accompanied each evening by several Christians from the Aomori church. Two of these, Mr Chiba* and Mr Kakizaki, both worked for the railway and therefore had something in common with Susumu Tamura.

After the meeting proper many would stay a while, sitting around in a circle on the old straw mats, talking informally and asking questions.

'Does the fear of death leave when one becomes a Christian?' asked one housewife, with tears in her eyes.

Such an open display of emotion in front of neighbors was unusual, and made quite an impression on the others, especially as the missionaries could then speak convincingly of how Christ has removed the sting of death for those who believe in Him. It wasn't long before this woman became a Christian.

Another, with unusual outspokenness for a Japanese, said, 'Perhaps it is impolite to say this, but the virgin birth, miracles and the Resurrection all sound like fairy tales to me.' This gave the Japanese Christians like Kakizaki the opportunity they were waiting for to answer such questions. Altogether it was a very friendly, informal time. Surprisingly, Umeno Tamura would sometimes quiz Michiko about her faith there. Perhaps this was to indicate to the neighbors that she herself didn't go along with this strange teaching, or because she was now secretly proud of her daughter. In any case it gave Michiko a wonderful opportunity to explain the Gospel in simple terms that all could understand.

Even Susumu seemed to enjoy the discussions with Kakizaki, although he claimed it was all nonsense. As headman of the village now, and the adopted son of a Buddhist temple official, he no doubt felt it would be very difficult to fulfil these responsibilities if he became a Christian.

Many were sorry when the week came to an end, and some of the women began to ask if there couldn't be a regular meeting in their village. The missionaries really had their hands full with outreach in the city, but Allen Fadel finally agree to come weekly if someone would open his home.

Guarded discussion followed, everyone secretly a little fearful of

---

*His story is told in *Captives of the Mighty* by Dorothy Pape (now out of print).

taking such a step. Michiko pulled her mother aside and whispered, 'Couldn't they meet in our house?'

'You know your father wouldn't like it,' came the reply. 'He didn't even want the house used for your sewing classes.'

Michiko prayed desperately. It seemed too good an opportunity to miss. At last, amazingly, Susumu himself said that since Michiko was responsible for starting the whole thing, it wasn't right for anyone else to be troubled with hosting the meeting and it should be held in their home!

So Allen began the weekly trips to Hamango. It wasn't bad at first, during the warm summer months. But as the icy fingers of winter gripped the province it was another matter..... First he had to travel in the cold train, then walk the mile of train track from Kominato station to Hamango. He had to time the walk carefully, too, so that he could step off the narrow single track onto a signal stand when an oncoming freight train was due.

Susumu sometimes travelled on the same train from work, and would be playing cards and gambling with fellow railwaymen. He obviously didn't want to be seen with this queer foreigner, and thought Allen must be a fool as he watched his tall figure bent against icy wind and blowing snow on the way to the house each week.

Once at the house, however, Allen got a warm welcome from Michiko's smiling face and from the two or three women who were now believers. Umeno Tamura too was becoming more friendly. 'Because these foreigners have shown so much kindness and interest in Michiko,' she thought, 'the least I can do is listen and try to understand what all the talk is about.' Also, she had never forgotten Michiko's apology that New Year's Eve, before telling them she was a Christian. Umeno knew it must be something really powerful which had changed Michiko so much, and couldn't deny that the change had lasted.

So it was not long before Umeno found she was beginning to understand what was said at the meetings, and to realize that there was a living Savior waiting to receive her. She hesitated no longer, and Michiko from then on had the immense joy of real Christian fellowship with her mother.

They prayed together for each member of the family. First they would pray for Taka, who would never come to the meetings but would close the paper doors and shut herself away in the other room until all the visitors had left.

They prayed for Ichiro, away at high school, who showed no interest in hearing about Christianity; and for young Shooji, still in primary school, who would occasionally come in to the meeting, but mostly preferred to stay in the other room with Taka. He was more independent now and refused to go to Michiko's children's meetings, except now and then with a few friends on purpose to tease the other children. In spite of this, he couldn't help noticing the different, happier atmosphere in the home because of Michiko's new influence, and the missionaries who visited them.

They prayed most fervently perhaps for Susumu, as head of the house. If he was home he would attend the meetings, but often he was working or would be late because of other commitments, accompanied by the customary drinking. He was never abusive, but would become very frank, humorous and open about his unbelief, evidently thinking he was making a favorable impression on others by good-humoredly poking fun at this fool of a foreigner.

Occasionally, if Allen had the opportunity to speak to him when he was alone and sober, he would say that it was impossible to become a Christian while his Buddhist mother was living. She would be terribly upset to think there would be no son to carry on the worship and offerings to the ancestors, believing her own spirit would also be cruelly neglected. The fact that he was an adopted son made his obligation even stronger, of course.

'You Christians say we shouldn't even have a *Butsudan* or *Kamidana*,' he protested. 'Why, these are absolutely part of our Japanese heritage and homes. The Obaa-san would be angry and terrified out of her wits at the very idea.'

In answer to Allen's questions he explained how the Emperor Temmu, back in AD 672, had decreed: 'My people shall make a place of honor in every home, and make it an altar.' In this place the Shinto worshippers had hung a scroll of the Sun-Goddess, while Buddhists placed a scroll or image of Buddha, and worshipped every day before this place of honor. In the course of time the Sun-Goddess had been put into a wooden box or shelf, the *Kamidana* (godshelf), and the images of Buddha were transferred to gilded boxes which ultimately became the *Butsudan* (Buddha altar).

In the Tokugawa era it became compulsory for everyone to be a Buddhist, and for Buddhist temples to hold various memorial services for the dead, while Christianity, regarded as evil and the enemy of the country, was forbidden for nearly two hundred years. Allen knew that during the recent war-time militarist regime State Shinto worship had been made compulsory, with even the subject Korean people being forced to place a *Kamidana* in their homes. So there was both the strength of law behind the custom, and also centuries of vague religious teaching which associated the spirits of the ancestors with these godshelves, the mortuary tablets, and the reading of *sutras*. Food and drink offerings had to be placed there daily to meet the needs of the spirits.

Susumu admitted that while most Japanese have real affection for their immediate, known ancestors, many also feel a deep fear that the spirits of the dead will hold a grudge against those fortunate enough to be still alive, and will follow them around threatening evil consequences unless they hold elaborate funerals and make frequent offerings.

'Some Buddhists teach that after thirty years few people will be left that the dead person has known,' he told the missionary. 'So then the spirit will cease its wanderings and human desires, and can enter the next world. That's why very important rites are observed on the 33rd anniversary of a person's death. There is even the rite of *In-nen kiri*, "cutting off the revenge of the ancestors," which priests will perform for a certain fee.'

With this ingrained fear of the displeasure of the ancestors, getting rid of the family *kamidana* and *butsudan* is the hardest test for many new Christians. It is particularly difficult for the eldest or only son to become a Christian. Hence Susumu Tamura's dilemma.

Those paper doors, however, had not kept the words of the Gospel from Taka's ears. At first Michiko and her mother frequently tried to explain things to her, but she stubbornly refused to listen, and at last when there appeared to be signs of approaching senility they gave up. Gradually Taka's old strength failed, and she sometimes became very irritable and difficult to care for.

One day, as the end seemed to be getting near, she suddenly announced to Umeno, 'You know, I'm going to heaven,' using the Christian, not the Buddhist term for heaven. Her daughter was busy sweeping the floor at the time, and thinking this was just the result of Taka's muddled mind she didn't take it seriously.

'Oh? Do you wish your bones to be placed with Father's at the temple?' she asked, to humor the old lady.

'No, with those who love the Lord Jesus,' she replied.

Umeno could hardly believe her ears. Her mother must surely be losing her mind! Was this the ardent Buddhist who had previously resisted all their efforts to talk to her about Christ?

She began to question Taka then, and with growing amazement discovered she knew nearly all the right answers. Michiko's teaching of the children in their home in Hamango, and Allen Fadel's weekly visits, together with their constant prayers, had evidently done their unseen work in her mother's heart.

The Tamuras were living in Aomori city by this time, so in great excitement Umeno sent for the pastor of the church. After talking with the old lady he, too, was convinced she was now truly believing in Christ.

'Do you wish to be baptized?'' he asked finally, and she gave a quick assent.

The pastor then carefully explained that the godshelf and Buddhist altar could have no further place in her room, or life. Both Umeno and the pastor were amazed at her response.

'Of course. Get rid of them. What use have they ever been?'

So those objects which had once been so highly, yet fearfully regarded, and which originally had been among the most expensive items of their post-war furnishings, were destroyed. Susumu, who was at work at the time, was not even consulted.

When he came home, old Taka pointed her finger at him and said, 'I want to see *you* in heaven, too!' This obviously made a great impression on him and his greatest obstacle to becoming a Christian was now removed. He began attending church, but it was actually another 18 months before he made a clear profession of faith, and also got the victory over his long-standing drink problem.

Not long after she had made her faith known, Taka passed peacefully away, and a Christian funeral was arranged at the church. This was something new for most people; since it is usually the younger ones in Japan who become Christians, funerals are not frequent.

One missionary present at the service described it as 'the most joyful funeral I've ever been at,' and went on 'Mrs Tamura told how Granny T had been converted, and how her husband had always felt he could never become a Christian while his mother was alive. But now she had surprised them by herself believing and getting rid of the godshelves first.'

The note of joy at a true Christian funeral because of the assurance of hope in Christ, is a great cause for astonishment to Japanese people when they experience it for the first time. When the lid of the coffin is removed so that relatives and friends may bid farewell to the one who has died, the peaceful expression on his or her face is always striking. Also the Scriptures and hymns have a joyful note of hope, in a language which can be understood. People join in the singing, instead of listening to priests chanting in Sanscrit or ancient Chinese.* So it is no wonder that those who gathered for Grandmother Tamura's funeral found it a remarkable experience.

The following Sunday they were still talking about it, and several gave testimonies of what it had meant to them. A man from a city bank, who had recently been attending church and seeking Christ, expressed real annoyance that he hadn't been informed of the funeral, so had been unable to experience all this the others were talking about! Soon afterwards he became a Christian, as did Susumu Tamura who, of course, was at the service.

So Taka Tamura, valiant hard-working pioneer of cold Karafuto, at nearly eighty years of age was willing to venture into another new country, the kingdom of God where she believed a loving Savior awaited her. And in her departing she was the means of at least two men drawing nearer that kingdom.

Susumu was not yet a member of it, however, and for Michiko her grandmother's death brought another heartbreaking encounter with him which revived her former bitterness. She too was now living in Aomori again, in a room across the city, and as soon as she heard the news of Taka's death she hurried over. But as she reached the outer door her father rushed out.

'Go away! There are many people here. It would have been better if you had not come!'

'But I want to see them, and grandmother for the last time. Please let me in,' Michiko pleaded.

'No, no! My supervisor from the railway is here to offer condolences, and many others. I can't let them see I have a daughter like you. They would be shocked. Go back! Go back!'

Michiko reeled beneath this unexpected blow. There was not only the deep personal wound, and sorrow at not seeing her grandmother, but also disappointment because she had hoped that her father, now attending services, was believing already. Stunned and blinded with tears, she swung herself falteringly on her crutches to the nearby railway station, and sank onto a bench.

She did not know how long she sat there, overcome with grief. As she cried desperately to God, however, she began to see at last that her father's feelings were natural in the circumstances. He had recently been transferred to an office job at Aomori station, since his sight had

*For a description of the contrast experienced by an ex-Buddhist priest, see Appendix 5.

been deteriorating and he had failed the safety test for train drivers. Of course he would want to appear at his best before his new supervisor.

'But I had hoped so much he was now a Christian, and it would have changed his feelings towards me..... Well, I must go on praying for him. God has done so many miracles for me, in opening up these amazing opportunities of service; He can certainly deal with my father', she thought.

Resolutely she stood up and got on the next train, back to her now widening field of service.

Chapter Thirteen

The Channel Broadens

WHAT WERE THESE WIDER OPPORTUNITIES now opening up for Michiko, and how had they come about? For some months after the meetings began in Hamango Michiko had rejoiced to see God working in her mother's life. Even her father was attending a few meetings and talking with the missionaries, and she felt an assurance that he too would one day become a Christian. Some of the neighborhood women and children were believing too. But gradually she began to feel restless in spirit, and found her thoughts often turning to the city again. She was so conscious of her own joy and changed mental attitude since becoming a Christian, and of the wonderful sense of being accepted and used by God in spite of her severely handicapped body, that she now began to have a new vision. This was to bring the Gospel to other handicapped people who were so often hidden away by their families, living a barren, useless life since no one would employ them.

The more Michiko thought about it, the more sure she became that this was what God wanted her to do next. But she had not the slightest idea how to go about it. She could only wonder, and pray.

Then the Aomori church planned a conference for Sunday School teachers and Michiko, of course, was eager to attend. She decided to take an early train into the city the day it was to begin, and visit the public library first to try to get some information about handicapped people in the city and province. But when she arrived at the library, Michiko couldn't resist first going along to the Religions section, to see if they had any books on Christianity which she hadn't read. After a few moments her eye joyfully caught sight of a book entitled *Confess Your Faith,* by Kanzo Uchimura, the founder of what came to be known as the Mukyokai (Non-church, or church-less movement).

Shifting her weight onto one crutch, Michiko reached out her free hand to take the book from the shelf; but just as she did so another hand reached for the same book.

'Oh! Excuse me! Do you want to read this, too?' asked a pleasant voice, and Michiko turned to see beside her a well-dressed girl, slightly younger than herself. She apologetically admitted she did, while the stranger looked her up and down for a second.

'Are you a Christian?' Seeing Michiko's smile, the girl continued, 'I am too, and would very much like to talk to you for a few minutes. Can you spare the time?' she asked eagerly.

Michiko readily agreed, and full of curiosity followed her to a seat. There she quickly learned the girl's name was Iwaeya and that her family was in business in Aomori. She was at present attending a famous Women's College in Tokyo and had become a Christian through contact with the Mukyokai there. She was especially interested to know Michiko because she had seen a school for training handicapped people in Tokyo, and was wondering about the possibility of starting one in Aomori when she finished college.

Michiko listened in awed amazement. Here surely must be an answer to her prayers for guidance! She told Iwaeya San what she herself had been thinking, adding that she would like to know a little more about the Mukyokai.

Iwaeya told her that Uchimura had become a Christian when he was one of the early students at the Hokkaido Agricultural College, which had been initiated with the help of a fine Christian man, Dr W S Clark of Massachusetts. Through an unfortunate experience of rivalry between the Methodist and Episcopal churches, Uchimura had soon started an informal, independent church there in Sapporo. Some years of study in the United States had not improved his opinion of highly-organized denominations, and on his return to Japan he eventually worked quite independently. By means of literature, lectures and small Bible study groups, he had by this time around 10,000 followers, the majority being from university circles.

Uchimura had now been dead for 25 years but his followers were still active, and it was they who had contacted Iwaeya San. While he had stressed doctrine very little, his main emphasis being on the living Christ, he had stated clearly: 'Conviction of sins, salvation by faith in the crucified Christ, and the hope of His coming — these are the three steps by which my soul was lifted to the joy and freedom of the heavenly vision.'

As the two girls talked they soon found that much of their belief was the same, that each had the same vision to bring Christ to the handicapped. Michiko even learned that Iwaeya San had been at high school with the girl who was now wife of the severely-crippled Mitsuhashi. She had trained as a nurse, and felt God calling her to marry him. Now she pulled him around in a small cart, or carried him on her back, so that he could have a much wider ministry as an evangelist.

'I shall graduate from college in March,' Iwaeya San said finally, when it was time for Michiko to leave for her meeting. 'Why don't you move back to the city, then we can work on this project together?'

Michiko prayed about this idea, wondering how it would be possible. In February she was very surprised to have a visit from a girl who had been in sewing school with her. 'A dressmaker in Aomori would like you to work for her,' she told Michiko, 'and she'll provide a room for you to live in. Will you come?'

Michiko felt this was the answer to her prayers and gladly agreed. A missionary couple, the Netlands, were now in Kominato, nurturing the little group of Christians into a church, and she felt assured she was no longer needed there. Allen Fadel offered to move her few possessions in his car — two pans, a charcoal burner to cook on, and a few cups and plates. At the end of March Iwaeya San returned to Aomori, but finding it impossible to get the financial help she had hoped for, she became a teacher at a mission school in Hirosaki, a smaller city less than an hour away by train.

Twice a week she and Michiko would meet after her return from school, have a bite to eat and then go to the city offices to look up the names and addresses of handicapped people. They found there were over 3,000 to contact, and for a whole year they visited, two evenings a week and again at the weekend. By the end of the year they were both feeling physically exhausted, so they began to write to an address first; if interest was shown, they would then plan a visit.

By this time the Christians in Aomori had left the kindergarten and built their own little church. So the two girls put their money together not only to mail letters, but also to pay for taxis to bring a few handicapped people to the church services. They also arranged periodic special meetings for the handicapped in a rented room, fearing it would not give a good impression to newcomers to see too many crippled people at once in the regular church services. Sometimes Michiko only ate one meal a day in order to pay for this.

As they began to get to know some of these people, their understanding grew of the many difficulties and sorrows they were experiencing, and Michiko appreciated more deeply the help she herself
had received from her family in the past. Nearly all these people, shut
away in their homes, had the same desire she had had to become
independent and to find some work they could do. So, when they left
the meetings and went home, they just became despondent again.

Michiko's heart went out to them, for she could understand so
well what life must be like for them. As she was reading her Bible one
day a verse struck her very forcibly. 'Hereby perceive we the love of
God, because he laid down his life for us; and we ought to lay down
our lives for the brethren' (1 John 3.16).

She knew that was God's message to her, and that somehow she
must 'lay down her life' on behalf of these handicapped friends. She
thought a moment and then closed her eyes.

'Thank you again, Lord, for giving your life for me,' she prayed.
'And help me to lay down my life for these people, with all their
problems.'

She kept on taking them to meetings, and telling them about
Christ...... then Michiko suddenly had another idea. *If only I could
have a place where they could come and work with me!* Eventually she
was sure that this was what she must do — open her own sewing
school, and have only handicapped girls as her students!

At the first opportunity she went home, eager to tell her family
her plans and enlist their help. But they did nothing but pour cold
water on her idea.

'You don't realize all the problems and responsibilities entailed in
such an undertaking, and especially with handicapped people,' her
father said impatiently.

'Why not try with ordinary girls first, then there wouldn't be so
much risk involved?' suggested her mother.

'But it's the handicapped ones who *need* the training! They're all
just cooped up at home there — you just don't understand how it
feels!' Michiko realized the indignation was rising in her voice, and
prayed for control.

'Of course we do! Haven't you been telling us what it's like most of
your life?' her father retorted. 'It needs healthy people, and people
with money, to start such a thing. It's not something a mere girl like
you can do. And we have neither the time nor the money.'

Michiko finally had to realize that her family now considered the
matter closed, and she tried not to show her anger and disappointment

in the remaining hours she was at home. As she sat in the train on her way back to Aomori, however, she felt the tears coming to her eyes as she stared out of the window. Quickly she prayed again for control, and as her eyes came to rest on Iwaki San, the familiar distant mountain looking like a miniature Mount Fuji as it rises from the flat rice fields, she remembered again that she was 'dug from the rock'. She wouldn't, couldn't give in.

'Lord, this is *your* idea. If nothing comes of it, if I fail, it's your responsibility,' she whispered.

On Sunday morning after the service Michiko asked to speak to the church leaders and told them of her idea. She could sense them looking her up and down, and though their eyes didn't dwell long on her legs she knew intuitively what their thoughts were. What could this poor cripple do?

They spoke more kindly and politely than her father. This would be a big undertaking of time and strength. And financially the church hadn't finished paying for its new building. It sounded a very good idea, but not really practicable yet.

So another wave of cold water was dashed against Michiko, but without shifting her purpose one bit. But how could it ever be fulfilled?

She was reading the book of Psalms just then, and one morning came to Psalm 18. Her heart warmed as she reached verse 6 and read: 'In my distress I called on the Lord: to my God I cried for help; He heard my voice from His temple, my cry before Him reached His ears.' At least this was an encouragement to go on praying.

She went on reading the particular circumstances of the psalmist and felt a little out of her depth, until suddenly her eyes lighted on a word full of meaning for her: 'Thou deliverest an afflicted people.....' Weren't those the very ones she was planning to help? And at His suggestion, she was sure.

Her eyes skimmed to the next verse.

'The Lord, my God, illumines my darkness.
     For by Thee I can attack a troop,
     And by my God I can leap over a wall.'

Michiko couldn't help laughing at that. The contrast between her limp, useless legs, and leaping over a wall was too ludicrous, too impossible!

Yet that was what it said — 'By my God I can leap over a wall.' By my God..... 'Lord, is it possible?' Michiko breathed. 'This problem is a wall, all right, an utterly impossible one for me to get over. But Lord, I will trust you.'

At work that day Michiko felt constrained to take a step of faith and make her project known.

'I've been thinking, I'd like to rent a big house and start a sewing school of my own,' she began.

The others opened their eyes in surprise. 'Really? How much money do you have?'

'I don't have any yet. But it's difficult for me to get around to make enquiries. If any of you hear of anything suitable, please let me know.'

A few days later one girl told Michiko she knew of an eight-mat* upstairs room nearby which was vacant, and the rent asked was reasonable.

The next evening Michiko and Iwaeya San went to look at the room.

'I'm sure it would do to start with,' panted Michiko, after she had managed to drag herself up the very steep narrow stairs. Japanese houses are always built to save as much space as possible.

'Are you sure?' her friend asked, looking at her anxiously.

'Yes, yes. But where are we to get the rent? We can't earn enough in the first month or two, not until the students get more experience.'

'I've saved enough to pay for the first two months. And listen! I could start an English class for children, after school,' exclaimed Iwaeya San. 'Many parents are wanting their children to learn English these days. Any money from that can go towards the project. This is just what I wanted to do!'

So the room was rented and Michiko, after much prayer and thought, wisely chose as her first students two girls who were a little less handicapped than she was herself. And the three of them pro-ceeded to live, cook, eat, sleep and work in that one upstairs room with a secondhand treadle sewing machine.

Soon her friends and previous acquaintances heard she was in business and brought work to her, and others begged to be allowed to come and learn. Sometimes it was a problem to find work for them all, and food to eat. 'Every day was a battle fought in prayer,' Michiko recalls. 'There were times when no food was left and I wondered what I would feed them for breakfast. But always our needs would be supplied in some way, and there would be food for breakfast.'

What brought the greatest joy to Michiko, however, was that both those first two students quite soon decided to become Christians.

*Each mat is six feet by three.

Sometimes they would all stop at an appropriate moment in their work and sing a hymn, or pray together. It was nearly all informal and unstructured, but those two girls really grew in grace and the knowledge of God, and both stayed in partnership with Michiko for a time after finishing their training.

It was soon after Michiko was well established in her little sewing school that her family moved to Aomori and grandmother Taka became a Christian. With this added joy, Michiko's heart was overflowing with gratitude for what God had done in her family, and for enabling her to jump over that seemingly impassable wall, the other side of which promised to be a channel for ever-widening blessing.

Chapter Fourteen

Michiko Proves an Answer to Prayer

IT WAS WHILE MICHIKO WAS OPERATING her first little sewing school that Allen Fadel came home from an afternoon of hospital visitation one day with a gleam of excitement in his eyes. Bessie Degerman, also a member of TEAM who lived next door, happened to be there chatting with his wife, Jane.

'Glad to see you here, Bessie,' said Allen. I have some news that may concern you! Would you believe it, I met a *gaijin* (foreigner) in the hospital today! A youngish woman, but one of the saddest-looking people I've ever met. I think it would be good if you and Jane could go visit her. She obviously didn't want to have anything to do with me.'

'Sure, I'll be glad to. What about tomorrow afternoon, Jane, would that suit you?'

'Yes, I think so, if Allen can stay with the children?'

'OK. Her name is Tani San, and she's in the women's medical ward. But that's all I can tell you about her.'

With some curiosity Jane and Bessie set out the next afternoon to the hospital. But the visit only served to deepen their wonder.

They found a woman of perhaps thirty, who looked quite western but only seemed able to speak Japanese. They learned she was in hospital for the treatment of some stomach ailment, perhaps ulcers. They agreed with Allen that she looked one of the most unhappy people they had ever seen. They had the impression she resented foreigners, yet they felt a special responsibility for her. But that day they could get very little information from her, so they read a few verses from the Bible and prayed, and then left after promising to return in a few days.

They visited several times, always having to make the conversation themselves, and concluding with reading and prayer. By this time they felt really curious, but most of all challenged to reach this unhappy woman for Christ; she was often in their prayers.

Then on one visit they were surprised to hear Tani San was soon to be discharged from the hospital, although she didn't look much improved to them.

They asked where she would be going, and after some hesitation she replied, 'I don't know.'

'Where is your home?'

'I have no home.'

'Well, what are you going to do?'

'I don't know,' Tani San repeated dully.

They could detect that tears were not far away. So this time, after choosing an appropriate Scripture, they prayed with added earnestness that God would reveal Himself to her, and provide the needed place to go for further recuperation.

As soon as they were outside the hospital they began to discuss this new turn of affairs..

'It's too bad she's leaving so soon, and we still haven't been able to get her to open up at all. Yet it did seem that the Lord had brought us in contact with her for a purpose,' Jane said in a puzzled tone.

Bessie hesitated a moment.

'You know, I feel so guilty living alone in that big house of the Kuels' meant for a family of six. The Japanese often remind me that many of them are still having to live a whole family in one room. I was wondering......'

Jane guessed what she was going to say.

'Well, that's an idea!' she exclaimed. 'Would you really be willing? I wonder how it would work out, though. You just might find yourself landed with her for good. And we really don't know a thing about her.'

'Yes, I know,' Bessie agreed. 'I'm scared all right! And yet the Lord seems to be telling me to do it, and to trust Him. Perhaps this is the thing that's really needed to get her to listen to the Gospel — a practical illustration that we really do care. Let's talk it over with Allen this evening.'

Later they all three prayed about it, and felt an assurance that Bessie should at least invite her to come. She looked so foreign, and as they were the only foreigners in the city it seemed they were the ones who should offer help.

So the next day they went to the hospital again, and gave the invitation. Tani San looked at them a moment in disbelief.

'Do you really mean that?' she asked at last.

'Yes, of course we do, we'll be glad to help until you feel stronger.'

Tani San thanked them sincerely, but her face didn't look any happier. It just seemed she had no interest in living at all.

The next morning Bessie got a spare bedroom ready, making it as bright and comfortable as possible. She put flowers on the bedside table together with a few books and magazines, including a Japanese New Testament.

When they got to the hospital they found that Tani San had all her worldly possessions there. But these were so few that they managed to get them, the woman herself, Bessie, Jane and two-year-old Mike Fadel all into a small Japanese taxi. Jane had had to bring Mike because there was no one to leave him with.

Once back home, Bessie did her utmost to be friendly and hospitable, but Tani San remained as withdrawn and despondent as she had been in the hospital, and would neither smile nor talk.

After a few days, while Tani San was having her afternoon rest, Bessie in desperation went over to see Jane.

'What can I do? She doesn't seem to be responding at all. It's just like talking to a brick wall! Do you have any ideas?'

'If only we knew *something* about her that would give us a clue,' murmured Jane in perplexity. She thought for a moment. 'You know, although the taxi was so crowded that day, I did see her glance at Mike several times. Perhaps it might help if she spent some time with the children. Look, why don't you both come over here for supper for a few days? That will at least give you a bit of a break and she just *might* respond more to the children.'

'Oh thanks! That'll be great! I really can't think of another thing to do myself. Let's just pray that this will work.'

After the first night or two Tani San really seemed to begin watching the four Fadel boys playing. Mike was at a particularly cute stage, and at last she gingerly began attempting to talk and play with him. Jane and Bessie noted this with excitement, and spent as long as possible in the kitchen doing the dishes so that Tani San would be alone with Mike.

This went on for several nights. At last, as Jane picked Mike up to take him to bed, she ventured to say, 'I can see you like little boys, Tani San.'

Suddenly there were tears in the woman's eyes.

'Yes — I had one once. He was killed when he was Mike's age.' Then she began to shake with violent sobs and would say no more.

Jane's and Bessie's eyes met. *So that's it,* they both thought.

Bessie put her arm around Tani San. 'I'm *so* sorry,' was all she could say, as she guided her guest home and put her to bed with a hot drink.

But that certainly wasn't the whole story and they still didn't know who Tani San really was. She wrote to no one, and received not a single letter.

Gradually, however, as she went to the Fadels' night after night, she began to add a little more about her past on the evenings when Allen was out at meetings, and the children were in bed. It was such a bitter, tragic story that it was no wonder she shrank from the pain of putting it into words. But as the warmth of the Christian family life at last began to penetrate her hard exterior, she finally felt able to share her story with them.

They learned her mother had been Australian and her father Japanese, though how they had met she did not say. Perhaps she had never known. The first thing she consciously remembered was that one day when she was six her mother had asked her whom she wanted to live with: her, or her father and grandmother. Of course she wanted to live with both, but since her grandmother made her favorite foods, she finally decided she would stay with her and her father. Her mother then departed, presumably for Australia, and was never seen again.

Soon after this, tragedy struck again for the little girl. Her father died, leaving her an orphan whom none of the relatives wanted to care for because she looked so 'American'. Usually in the children of mixed marriages the darker coloring is dominant, but in Tani San's case it was not so. By this time war had been declared on the Western Allies (which may have been the reason for the break up of the marriage), and so at school she was constantly and mercilessly tormented because of her foreign looks and the color of her hair and eyes.

Her life was utterly miserable in those growing-up years. But when the war was over she went to Tokyo to work, and there met a young man to whom she was happily married for a few years. They had a little son. Her happiness was short-lived, however, for when the child was two and a half years old he was out for a walk with his father one day, and both were knocked down by a car and killed.

Tani San became numb with grief. What could she do? Where could she go? She knew she couldn't live with her in-laws, for from the beginning they had never approved of their son marrying this foreign-looking freak.

Her one thought was to get as far away as possible from that place of tragedy, so she bought a train ticket to Aomori, in the extreme north, where she did any kind of odd job she could get. Soon, however, she became sick and was in and out of hospitals for the six years she had been there. She had made no friends.

When the missionaries had first spoken to her about the love of God, she had not been able to believe it. If God was a God of love why had He let all these cruel things happen to her? She especially hated her mother for leaving her, and instinctively disliked all foreigners because she had been tormented so much for looking like one; this again she figured was her mother's fault.

Gradually, however, Tani San began to respond to the love she was experiencing from Bessie and the Fadels, and in time opened her heart to receive Christ. She started to smile and to talk a little more, and gained some weight, although she still remained a heavy smoker.

When she had been with Bessie about six weeks she began talking about getting a job. 'I feel strong enough now, and I don't want to be a burden to anyone,' she told Bessie. She had begun attending church and enjoyed it very much, so now she wished she could find a place where she wouldn't have to work on Sundays. But this seemed most unlikely since she was only fitted for the sort of unskilled jobs that were usually seven-day-a-week ones.

'Nothing is impossible with God, Tani San,' Bessie assured her. 'So we will both pray that He will supply you with a job and place to live where you won't have to work on Sundays.'

Tani San shook her head in unbelief. After all, she had had six years' experience of trying to get jobs in Aomori. But she started to pray.

Perhaps the matter was mentioned at the church prayer meeting, too. In any case, just a few days later a beaming Michiko Tamura appeared on the Fadels' doorstep, and said she would like to speak to Bessie too.

'I've come to ask whether you think it would be possible for Tani San to live and work with me at my sewing school,' she told them with a smile. 'She can be my legs. It will be a big help to have her deliver the finished work, do some of the cooking and shopping, and so on.'

The Fadels thought it was a wonderful idea and Bessie excitedly went across to get Tani San.

When she heard the invitation from Michiko's own lips, Tani San was overjoyed at the offer, and at the knowledge that God had heard her prayers. She was actually going to be able to continue living with Christians! She could hardly believe it!

So the move was made. By now the little sewing school had a few other handicapped students attending daily, and was taking orders from a big department store. So they were able to support Tani San as a member of the staff. It meant there were now four girls living in that one eight-mat room, but somehow they managed to do it happily, all growing as Christians, and working hard as well, as a testimony of their faith. For the first time in her life Tani San felt really accepted by other Japanese. It was in fact a big help to them to have her buy and prepare food, buy some of the sewing supplies and deliver the finished work. In this way they themselves could do more sewing.

Just one problem remained, however. Tani San was still a slave to cigarettes, for they had been her only solace through all those years of sorrow and loneliness. No one objected, or criticized her, but Michiko prayed about it and then thought of a plan. In the summer she'd take Tani San to camp for the entire adult program.

Out at the lovely quiet spot by the ocean, Tani San listened without distraction to the talks on a deeper spiritual life, and her faith was strengthened. One day she smoked her last cigarette, and her joy then was very real. She smiled and talked gaily, and gave public testimony to her faith and the victory Christ had just brought into her life.

The following November the Aomori church planned a baptism service and Tani San asked to be a candidate. At that time it was too cold to have it in the ocean, of course, and as the little church had no baptistry they rented for the occasion one of the public baths at a hot-spring resort hotel, not far from the city. Here, along with several others, Tani San demonstrated both symbolically and by her words of testimony that she had indeed died to the old life, and was now a new creature in Christ. The girls at the sewing school had shown their love and support by making her a lovely new kimono to wear after the baptism.

In spirit Tani San was indeed a new person, but her poor physical body had apparently been damaged irreparably in those years of hardship, neglect and perhaps an overload of nicotine. By Christmas she was back in hospital and this time cancer of the breast was diagnosed.

She was operated on and returned home, but soon it was obvious the disease had spread. Bessie Degerman had been transferred to work in Tokyo, so could not help now, but Michiko and the other girls lovingly cared for Tani San for several months. When she became bed-ridden a new problem arose, for theirs was an upstairs room and the toilet was downstairs. Daphne Kelly, OMF missionary nurse who had taken over Bessie's Bible class which the girls attended, recalls the loving hilarity with which the three crippled girls wrestled with the problem of getting themselves, crutches, and the old tin bedpan down those very narrow, steep stairs. During that time too the man in the next room went away for a few days leaving his transistor radio on full blast, and they had to endure this around the clock until the battery was used up.

As the cancer invaded her gall bladder and liver, Tani San was unable to keep anything down and had to be moved to hospital. One day when Daphne was visiting her she asked the patient if there was anything she would really like.

'Ice cream,' came the unhesitating reply. Umeno Tamura, who was now helping to care for her in the hospital, at once offered to go and buy some. 'No, no,' Tani San said, 'I meant the home-made kind.'

Evidently she had had some at the Fadels' or Bessie's, and remembered how good it tasted compared with the local variety. Daphne hurried home and got her Canadian fellow-worker, a dietician, to make some, and took it back in a thermos bottle. But even that wouldn't stay down.

In October, as the fall leaves were brightening the trees outside in preparation for the barrenness of winter, Tani San rallied a little after a period of desperate suffering. She decided to make plans for her funeral service, which she wanted to be a triumphant one.

As required in crowded Japan, she would have to be cremated, but she decided to wear the good kimono which she had been given to celebrate her baptism, not some old garment which it was customary to put on a corpse.

In a few days she was gone. Before the funeral service, when neighbors came to pay their respects, the church people would say, 'Please don't bow to the body. Tani San isn't here, she's with the Lord Jesus.' Those ignorant of Christianity looked startled, and some bowed to the coffin anyway. But, as at Taka's funeral, there was joyful singing, including Tani San's best-loved hymns, the reading of her favorite 23rd Psalm and the opportunity to explain to all those present the hope of eternal life that believers have in Christ.

Umeno Tamura particularly, with help from a few other ladies from the church, had been indefatigable in caring for Tani San in the hospital, where much is left for relatives to do. Now she and Susumu, with true Christian compassion, took the place of her relatives. After the coffin has passed through the oven at the crematorium, the relatives have the gruesome task of picking up the remaining bones with a special pair of large chopsticks, and putting them in the box or urn brought along to receive them. Sometimes this involves crushing them down in the box to make room for the skull. This is regarded as part of one's responsibility in loving and caring for one's own family, but is not something one would willingly do for others.

Then there could have been a real problem about the burial, for all graveyards in Japan are Buddhist, and this can prove a great difficulty for Christians. In some places, new groups of Christians have been known to buy a burial plot even before building a church.

Susumu Tamura, once he finally became a convinced Christian, showed great discernment in the matter of ancestor worship and Buddhist culture, and had already bought a small piece of land for a family burying ground. Taka's ashes were there and he now offered a space for Tani San's remains. Here they buried her as if she were one of the family, amid thanksgiving that she was now released from all the suffering which had filled so much of her life, and could rejoice in the presence of her new Savior and Lord.

Three days before she died Tani San had called Michiko to her bedside and said she had something to tell her.

'Tamura San, be at peace. Everything will be all right. After three years I believe God is going to give you a bigger place. Only look straight ahead. They put blinkers on horses so they can't see to the left or right,' and Tani San weakly raised her hands to the side of her face to demonstrate. 'Don't look around. Only look ahead, and look up, and keep going.'

This was to be an encouragement that Michiko sorely needed in the months ahead.

Chapter Fifteen

House of Grace

MICHIKO AND HER STUDENTS had been so busy attending to Tani San's needs first at home and then visiting the hospital every day, that somehow they had just about given up working. Now after her death there was no money for the rent and other expenses, and indeed the blow of losing her was so great that it seemed best for them to close up completely for a short time and move from the place which had so many memories of her, while they regained their physical strength and emotional equilibrium. Michiko was also concerned about her brother, Shooji, at this time. He had caught tuberculosis in high school and was often hospitalized.

After a little rest at her parents' house, however, Michiko's resilient spirit recovered, and a month later she was looking for another room. Eventually she found one, not far from the house her family had rented when they moved to the city. Here two girls who had become students just before Tani San's hospitalization joined her again. They were not Christians at first, but soon responded to the Gospel and developed a deep and lasting friendship with Michiko. One of them, Mi-se Yanagizawa, married a crippled man after some years and, though glad for her, Michiko really missed her. The couple's happiness was complete when a child was born to them, but soon afterwards the husband suddenly died. Thanks to Michiko's training, however, Mi-se was able to support herself by taking in sewing.

The other, a sweet-faced girl named Ryoko Matsumoto, continued much longer with Michiko, and helped her in a distant adventure which was to have far-reaching and utterly unimagined consequences for them both.

Meanwhile in this new room Michiko continued her former practice of informal devotions and singing, and occasionally arranged evangelistic meetings there. Perhaps it was because of this that the landlord told her he would not renew the contract at the end of the year. What was she to do now? Day after day Michiko puzzled over the problem, asking God to show her His solution. She remembered Tani San's words, but just did not know where 'ahead' was now. If God would show her, she would follow.

Then one day, with a little gasp at the seeming impossibility of it, Michiko suddenly realized what the answer was. Here was certainly another wall she could only leap over with God's help! They must now build a place of their own, somewhere more convenient for the needs of the handicapped, and where there would be no restrictions on singing and having meetings.

'But I have no money,' she thought, 'and Iwaeya San won't be able to help now she is married and has a baby. Where can the money come from?' Michiko talked to the Lord again:

'If this idea is from You, then You must do the supplying, Lord. I'm willing for whatever You want.'

The Netlands were back in the area again, so she consulted them. 'My rented room is too small,' she told them, 'and we will lose it at the year-end anyway. Many handicapped girls still want to come, so I feel we must have a place of our *own,* big enough to train at least eight at a time.'

Convinced now of Michiko's ability both to run a sewing school and to win girls to Christ, the Netlands gave her every encouragement. They also promised to try to get financial help for the project from friends.

Next Michiko went to her father and rejoiced to find him, too, sympathetic. In fact he and Umeno were now really proud of what their daughter had managed to accomplish. He had recently borrowed money to buy land in the city suburbs where he planned eventually to build a house. Now he calculated that he wouldn't need all the land for his house, and finally said that if Michiko could raise the money for the building, she might put it on part of his land.

When the church members heard about the project, they were also enthusiastic, some offering a little money and others their labor. The Netlands received a few hundred dollars from friends in the USA, but the rest of the money came from Japanese, even from some non-Christians. As more and more people heard about the project it was written up in the local paper, and even mentioned on television. A handicapped girl prepared to do so much for others seemed to touch people's hearts and soon, with the promised voluntary labor, there was enough money to start building.

It was to be a three-roomed house, quite a luxury after living and working for so long in one room. But Michiko wanted eight resident girls, and opportunity for others from the neighborhood to come daily. When the roof went up a Christian thanksgiving ceremony was held instead of the pagan rites and drinking, customary in eastern countries. Michiko named her new home *Megumi no Ie* (House of Grace), and prayed that God's grace would indeed reach many handicapped girls there.

The one disadvantage of the new house was that it was on the growing edge of the city, too far from the church for the handicapped to get there easily. So Mr Kamikazawa was invited to hold services at the House of Grace. He was a fine Christian from the nearby leprosarium, whose disease had been arrested, and he had been the means of many fellow sufferers finding new life in Christ.

The newspaper and TV coverage resulted in people outside the city hearing of the project, and again Michiko couldn't accommodate all who wanted to come. One day a letter arrived from a woman in a coastal town further south, who said she was a Christian, badly paralysed with TB of the bone. Although bedridden she had full use of her hands, and wanted this training so much.

Michiko was very moved by this, but had serious misgivings. 'She will be unable to use a sewing machine — such a vital tool to the others' she pondered, — 'and after caring for Tani San we know what it means to have someone dependent on a bedpan. But I'd really like to be able to help this poor woman. What a difficult life she must have! Perhaps she could at least do some of the finishing, button-sewing and similar jobs.' Finally Michiko agreed to accept her on trial, and she actually stayed two years, until her health deteriorated further.

At the House of Grace Michiko was able to experiment with leg braces, and found they gave her much more stability, so that she was able to stand if she could lean against something, and thus have both hands free from her crutches. It was some years after the war that such 'luxury' items began to be produced, but at last Michiko was able to take advantage of some of the new devices. She had tried a wheelchair before, but models were still big and clumsy, and so unsuitable for a Japanese house that she had given up in frustration.

Even with the added help of braces and the convenience of her new home, it was a struggle to care for this woman who had to lie prone most of the time. Fortunately she could write well, so Michiko passed on the task of corresponding with shut-ins which she herself had been doing since the first sewing school began. She also subscribed to the magazine *Gospel for the Millions,* and in it saw the needs of other shut-ins: those in hospitals and prisons, and the elderly as well as handicapped, who would like to receive used copies of the magazine.

One day a letter came from a prisoner in southern Japan. A friend had received the magazine and passed it on to him, and he now wanted to know more about Christianity. Delighted, Michiko got the bedridden lady to send another magazine and tract. Month by month these were sent, and when the prisoner continued to express interest Michiko began to add a personal note of encouragement.

Eventually, to her great surprise, Michiko got a letter from a prison official asking if she would write again to this man. He was in the death-row cells, and might not have long to live. Full of concern, she wrote with added urgency, expressing the truth of the Gospel as clearly as she could.

'After a year of reading Christian literature he can't be far from believing,' she thought. 'If only I could talk to him!' Then the idea came, 'Perhaps I could visit him? Then surely he would accept Christ, and be sure of eternal life after his execution.' The journey would take nearly 24 hours, by crowded express trains, but Michiko didn't consider the difficulty and discomfort it would involve for her. Instead she wrote to ask the official if a visit was possible.

The reply came in a few days.

'The only woman visitor a condemned prisoner may have is his wife. Would you consider being married to him?'

Michiko was shocked to the core, and at first dismissed the idea as ridiculous. Then she received a letter from the prisoner's elder sister, asking her the same thing. Again she refused to take it seriously. Eventually the prison official wrote again explaining that death sentences were being commuted to life imprisonment. 'This prisoner is a good man,' Michiko read, 'and if he could be married, even only on paper, it would be a great encouragement to him to improve his life. You would be able to visit him......'

It was still an impossible-sounding suggestion, and yet now Michiko really had to begin thinking and praying about it. She suddenly wondered if it might even be an answer to some other urgent prayers. At that time she had a few really pretty young girls as students, and was finding them more and more difficult to handle. Social conditions were changing and these girls had boyfriends who came to take them

out in the evenings. In spite of being told to be back at 10 p.m., they
sometimes stayed out till midnight or even 1 a.m. and she grew very
worried. Their parents would hold her responsible if anything happened to them, and she was afraid these men might take advantage of the
girls being slightly disabled, and then not marry them in the end.

However, when she remonstrated with the girls they said she was
jealous of them because she had no boyfriend and couldn't get married.
They became rebellious and refused to listen to the Bible or come to
meetings. Michiko felt at her wits' end. She got up at four o'clock on a
number of mornings, and went near the ocean, crying to God to show
her what to do.

Could these letters from the prison somehow be God's answer, so
that the girls would understand and respect her more? Yet how could
she tell them, and still keep it secret from her family? Michiko was
quite sure what the family's reaction would be. Most marriages in
Japan are arranged by a go-between, and while there is usually a
Shinto ceremony, the legal part just consists of entering the new name
on the family record at the local ward office. Some husbands, in fact,
don't register their wife's name until she has borne a son (though the
wife probably doesn't know this). Families with daughters but no sons
would try to get a husband to come into the family and take the wife's
name. That is what Michiko would have to do, but her father's anger
at the idea of including a convicted criminal on their family register
could well be imagined. 'But does that really matter?' she wondered.
'Here is a human being, perhaps not long for this world, and close to
God's kingdom if only someone were there to help him.' She struggled
with conflicting thoughts and fears, and after much prayer at last
became convinced that in the circumstances this was the right thing to
do.

Next there was the journey to consider. Michiko knew it would be
impossible for her to accomplish alone, so next morning she called
Riyoko Matsumoto aside into the little kitchen, while the others were
busy in the workroom.

'Riyoko San, how would you like to go on a trip down south?'

'What do you mean?' Riyoko stared in astonishment.

'You know that prisoner we have written to, and prayed for so
much?'

'That one who is to be executed for murder?'

'Yes. I had a letter from one of the officials the other day, and it
suggested I should go see him as his wife. So I'm thinking of entering
his name on our family record as my husband, and then going to see

him.'

'Michiko San! You do think of the wildest things!' exclaimed
Riyoko. 'Your family will be terribly angry. Are you sure this is the
right thing to do?'

'Yes,' Michiko answered seriously. 'I've prayed about it and I
believe God wants me to influence this man for Christ. He really seems
to be seeking, and there's no possibility of him ever coming out of
prison. I can easily remove his name afterwards. Anyway, my family
have told me so many times they could never find a husband for me, so
what would it matter? Will you come?'

Riyoko thought a moment. Although she had a deformity, she
wasn't as crippled as Michiko, and as she didn't need crutches herself
she would be able to help her friend on this long journey which would
be hard on both of them. As she met Michiko's pleading gaze, Riyoko's
heart softened. After all, she did owe her both her present employable
skills and above all her Christian faith.

'All right,' she said at last. 'It sounds really crazy, but I'll come.'

Her mind made up, Michiko quickly went about her preparations.
She completed the entry in the family record, and then merely announced that she and Matsumoto San were going down south to visit
one of their contacts.

The long, crowded train journey was torture for them both, but
Michiko's thoughts and prayers were all on the mission before her.
Changing stations in Tokyo for the south-bound train was a trying
experience amid the crowds rushing up and down the steps to the
connecting subway line, and Michiko was very thankful for the new
leg braces which made her less helpless than formerly.

At last they reached their destination and telephoned the official
who had written to Michiko. Soon a black car with two policemen
arrived to take them to the prison. Michiko was shocked and dis-
appointed to learn the usual visiting time was only ten minutes! The
warder seemed to assume from her correspondence that she was an
evangelist, however, and said she could have thirty minutes with the
prisoner. A guard was detailed to go with her and she hurried after
him, as fast as her crutches would allow, to the room where she would
meet her husband for the first time.

It was a strange and potentially embarrassing situation, but Michiko
was so much in earnest that she had no time to think of lesser things.

She saw a man of about her own age, with what would have been
a pleasant face if he hadn't had such a hopeless expression. She wasted
no time saying anything about herself, but with her usual sweet,

outgoing manner opened her Bible at John's Gospel and began to read and explain as many verses as she could.

The guard was present all the time, writing down what she said, while the prisoner answered mostly in monosyllables. In no time at all, it seemed, the thirty minutes was gone. The prisoner only bowed formally in farewell, but Michiko was sure that she had seen a spark of interest in his downcast eyes.

Back at the warder's office, she asked if any religious workers visited the prison.

'Yes,' he replied. 'A Buddhist priest, Catholic priest and an Episcopal clergyman.' Michiko hesitantly requested permission to phone the latter, and the warder readily agreed. The clergyman did not give her much encouragement, however. He told her he just went to address a whole group and did not have contact with individual prisoners. Nor did he want it, she suspected.

'Is there no one else?' she asked the warder in deep disappointment.

'No, those are the only ones who come regularly, I think, ...wait a minute, though. I believe there is one other. But he doesn't dress like a priest.'

'Oh, I wish I could talk to him,' Michiko said wistfully. She somehow felt a human contact would mean much more to this prisoner than just printed material, but she wanted to be sure it would be someone who could explain the Gospel.

'Well, let's see if we can find him,' responded the unusually helpful official. He shuffled through some papers. 'Here it is. His name is Uetaki. I'll see if there is a car free to take you.'

Soon Michiko found herself talking to the fairly young, dynamic pastor of a Holiness church in the city. Assured he was a real believer, Michiko told him of her contact with this prisoner, and begged him to visit him.

The pastor willingly agreed and Michiko returned to their lodgings with a lighter heart. The prison car then took them back to the station and this unusual kindness and interest gave Michiko added assurance she had done the right thing in coming, however questionable it might seem to others.

She had learned that the man's family was still appealing for a retrial, since he had been convicted on circumstantial evidence only. Because of good conduct he was eventually granted training as a skilled cabinet maker, and subsequently became a supervisor in that department of the prison workshops. Meanwhile Michiko decided to repeat the visits every six months, and before long it seemed certain that her husband was truly trusting in Christ.

The pastor kept in touch, and welcomed the two girls on their twice-yearly visits. In fact, one wonderful and unexpected result of the whole matter was that he eventually arranged a marriage for Riyoko with a Christian man there. While Michiko regretted losing a second valued friend, she felt this was further confirmation she had done the right thing.

This encouragement was timely, for one day her father discovered the new name on the family record and was understandably furious. Michiko could only apologize, and say it was the only way to ensure this poor man became a Christian; but her father was so upset that he never forgave her until just before his death. This new estrangement from him hurt her very much.

Michiko continued her many avenues of service; faithfully supporting the church, helping in Sunday school, writing to shut-ins, and having the full responsibility of teaching, feeding and generally caring for her students. Her witness continued to bear fruit in some lives, though not all responded to the claims of Christ. With both of her original helpers gone, Michiko was left with added responsibilities, and felt keenly the loss of strong Christian fellowship in the work. But with characteristic determination she did her best to make the House of Grace live up to its name, and the school also had a good reputation for the quality of its work.

OMF missionary Anne Friesen had a kimono made there to wear at home on deputation work. She was most impressed by the way one of the girls, in spite of being very lame, was determined to go with her to buy the material, to make sure it was correct for a person of her age, and also insisted that the *obi* (sash) and sandals must be exactly right to go with it. When Anne wore the kimono at various meetings in Canada she would tell where it was made, and give vivid details about the House of Grace and its ministry. The Netlands, Fadels and other missionaries who knew Michiko were also telling about the House of Grace in America and Australia.

The day was not far distant too when she, who was once shut away in closets so as not to embarrass or disgust her father's guests, was actually driven to the big US Air Force base at Misawa, in Aomori prefecture, to be guest speaker at a meeting of the Protestant Women of the Chapel. By means of an interpreter, she shared the story of how God had changed her life and enabled her to serve Him, and thus became a channel for further blessing to many who heard her there.

But no one knew of the special blessing she had been to an unknown prisoner, almost a thousand miles from her home.

Chapter Sixteen

A Larger Vision and Long-delayed Victory

NOT FOR LONG WAS MICHIKO CONTENT with her achievements at the House of Grace. Once more she began to experience that restlessness of spirit which she had come to associate with God's call to prepare for something new.

'What I am doing is too small, and too slow,' she realized eventually. 'There are still so many handicapped people in the city and the surrounding areas, whose needs are not being met.' Yet with responsibility for the food, health and counselling of her resident students, her time and energy were already so committed that she could not possibly teach a larger number.

Slowly the answer began to come: something really big this time, so that others could be responsible for the catering, housekeeping and physical care, while she gave herself to teaching sewing, counselling and evangelism. An exciting prospect, but how could it ever be achieved? Further expansion was impossible on her father's property, because he had built a nice house there now. It could only mean a new start in another location.

When the plan became clear in her mind she discussed it first with the missionaries, and then with her family. They were unanimous. It was not possible. It was too big a responsibility, financially and in every way. The church leaders were equally dubious, although they did form a committee of Christian businessmen to investigate the feasibility of such a scheme. The committee's report was depressing. It was now 1967; prosperity and inflation had already begun to shoot prices up, and the cost of land and building on the scale she envisaged appeared completely out of reach.

The wall of opposition this time truly seemed impassable, and

Michiko was deeply discouraged. In the midst of this she went back again to that verse in the Psalms which had meant so much to her before. Certainly it could only be by God's power that she could leap this obstacle. 'Lord, if this is your plan, help me to jump,' she pleaded. Then she felt free at least to talk about the need to others.

One of the students at the school just then was the daughter of a man who owned a considerable piece of farm land in an area called Kobata, which the spreading city was now turning into a suburb. Development was already beginning there, including the building of a new university, and one day this girl went with her father to inspect his property, and have a look at the university building going up.

As they stood on his land she suddenly said, 'Father, please don't sell this to anyone. I would like to have it.'

'What on earth can you do with it?' he asked, astonished.

'The teacher at the sewing school is needing land because she wants to build a much bigger place for the handicapped,' explained his daughter. 'She's been so kind, and has helped us so much, I'd like her to be able to help many more people.'

'H'm. How much would she need?' he asked.

'About 300 tsubo.'*

'Very well,' her father said finally. 'I will keep 300 tsubo. The price for her will be 1,000 yen a tsubo, to be paid as she can manage it.' (About 3 dollars U.S. per square foot then.)

This was certainly cheap, and Michiko saw it as God's wonderful provision. But she didn't even have that amount of money, and certainly nothing with which to begin building.

As Japan's industry developed, and the country grew more prosperous with a higher standard of living, different levels of the government were at last beginning to feel more responsibility for the sick and handicapped. Some friends suggested that Michiko should ask the city to be responsible for the building she wanted. She was doubtful about that. 'Would I have freedom to present the Gospel?' she wondered. 'After all, that is the most important reason for having the school.'

One day a man Michiko used to know in Kominato heard about the land that had been offered to her. He had already started a printshop for men who were handicapped, largely from TB, and they too were outgrowing their premises. So he arranged to meet Michiko. 'Why don't we go in together?' he suggested. 'Perhaps then we might qualify for a sizable government grant.'

---

*A *tsubo* is about four square yards.

'That might be possible,' Michiko said, 'so long as you understand that the most important thing for me is to present Jesus Christ to my students.' At first the man impatiently tried to dissuade her, but she insisted that was ultimately their greatest need. The talks continued at intervals, and as Michiko remained adamant the man at last realized she really meant what she said.

'All right,' he finally gave in, 'I agree that you can have complete freedom to do as you like, if it's really so important to you.'

By this time, however, the city had begun to take an interest and decided they wanted to build a Rehabilitation Colony for the handicapped. Since Michiko and this man were already experienced and successful in such work, the city naturally thought they would be a big help in the new project. So Michiko became involved in more and more discussions, and it seemed there was constant hassle as the different people involved argued over the issues.

Through all this time the other Christians in Aomori gave Michiko very little support, because they were against her getting involved in working with non-Christians. It was a most difficult and painful time for her, and her only comfort was in God and His word. Chapters 14 and 15 of John's Gospel became especially precious to her then. 'Let not your hearts be troubled. You believe in God, believe also in me.' And 'If you ask anything in my name, I will do it. If you love me, you will keep my commandments.' She remembered, too, the words which had meant so much to her when she first decided to give herself to be a channel of blessing to others. 'This is my commandment, that you love one another as I have loved you. Greater love has no man than this, that a man lay down his life for his friends. You are my friends if you do what I command you.'

So Michiko stood her ground. 'I must have freedom to hold Christian meetings if the Colony is to be built on my land, and if I am to work there,' she maintained. Eventually, after months of talk, an agreement was reluctantly, yet miraculously reached. The land became the property of a Board of Directors, of whom Michiko was to be one, and they in turn would be responsible to the government Social Welfare Department. As well as heading up the sewing section, now able to accommodate 45 students, Michiko was also to be supervisor of the women's side of the work. When the first building was completed, Michiko's stipulation was respected, and Anton Netland was asked to hold a Christian service of dedication, and was able to hold some evangelistic meetings there.

Michiko found it a wonderful relief to be rid of the burden of some of her former responsibilities, such as providing salaries, food and sick care for the girls living in her home. Now these were all the responsibility of the government. Her vision for the employment of many more handicapped people was partially fulfilled too, in that the office, kitchen and maintenance staff at the Colony were almost all either slightly handicapped themselves, or had relatives who were and therefore knew how to meet their needs in a caring way.

Problems were not ended, however. After a time some of the aggressive new religious sects demanded that if the Christians were allowed to hold meetings there in a government institution, they must be allowed the same opportunity. It was hard to refuse this argument.

Michiko was very troubled. Was what her Christian friends had forecast to become a reality, in spite of her long, hard fight to prevent it? Once again she sought wisdom from God. 'Don't let this all come to nothing, Lord. It was for your sake I did this, wanting to reach more people for you. Show me what you want me to do now.'

Across the street from the main entrance to the Colony there was still a small piece of vacant land. This caught Michiko's eye one day, and gave her the inspiration she needed. She would build her own house! On that site, it would be off the Colony premises yet so close that anyone who wanted could easily slip across to talk about Christ.

It meant borrowing some money, but Michiko went ahead and soon had the comfortable little home in which I met her. It is just a few steps on her crutches — down the garden path, across the street, in through the main gate to the offices on the right, and the sewing department is just a little further along the hall. With a telephone extension in the sewing room and her own phone at home, Michiko is saved many steps these days, and 'Tamura Sensei' is readily available for any of the girls who need her counsel.

Twice already the original buildings at the Colony have been added to, and each time Anton Netland has been invited to speak at the dedication ceremonies, presenting Christian truth.

By the time I visited Michiko in May 1977 a further whole new five-storey building was almost finished. It was to be chiefly devoted to the printing works, but also with the most up-to-date living quarters for the handicapped, with specially equipped bathrooms, a dining room with automatically opening doors, and everywhere suitable for wheelchair traffic. This is only the second such colony in Japan, and now there are around two hundred residents. Some just come for a short time to learn a trade, but many of the severely handicapped remain there permanently, doing a full-time, productive job. Now over a thousand have received training there.

Although many handicapped people have no financial worries these days, they still have what Michiko calls 'luxury problems'. 'Will I ever get married?' is a common one, and there are cases like the deaf-mute girl whose story is told in the Introduction. Michiko herself now earns her living expenses by teaching, and can eat her main meals already prepared in the Colony dining room. So she has more peace of mind and free time to witness to and counsel the girls out of school hours in her own home.

In her usual winsome way, she also soon began to draw some of the neighborhood children to her home to what became a Sunday school class, and then later started a weekly Bible study class for adults.

Working for the government gave Michiko an unexpected and wonderful opportunity of which she was quick to take advantage. Characteristically, she was the very first handicapped person in the area to learn to drive a car. It had to be a specially equipped one, of course, with all hand controls. She had to learn in the evenings after work and, according to her mother, she lost quite a bit of weight in the month she took to complete the course!

It happened to be winter, too, and as soon as she had passed the test there was a heavy fall of snow. When she was out alone for the first time, the car suddenly skidded and dropped down a bank about six feet below the road.

She had still been within sight of the Colony when it happened, and so the car had been seen disappearing down the bank. Several people hurried across and looked down anxiously.

'She's not dead!' was their first relieved comment.

Somehow Michiko managed to get out of the car, and it was later hauled up on the road again. She was not put off by this experience, and continued driving. Heavy snow frequently falls in Aomori, so she always carries a shovel in the car, and with her usual determination somehow manages to kneel and shovel away any snowdrift she happens to get stuck in.

After her courageous example, three other handicapped staff learned to drive, and the Colony now has several of these specially equipped cars and station wagons. They are of incalculable value, not only for transporting the crippled people, but also for getting supplies. Michiko especially found it an advantage to be able to go herself to get the materials and colors needed for orders for the sewing department, especially as the Colony is in a newly-developed area with few stores nearby.

Such freedom of movement, and the sense of independence it brought, must have been very sweet indeed to one who had been handicapped so long. Seeing her sitting at the wheel and confidently handling a car, one would have no idea that she is crippled.

Another matter, too, brought very special joy to Michiko after she was well settled at the Colony. It was in fact the answer to years of prayer. Her younger brother Shooji had completed his high school course in spite of TB, and immediately after he graduated his doctor had arranged an operation for him at a hospital for railwaymen and their dependents at Sendai, about halfway to Tokyo. Here a Christian doctor had begun a weekly Bible study, and largely out of boredom Shooji decided to go, especially since his friends at home wouldn't know. After a couple of weeks he realized he already knew quite a bit about the Bible from what Michiko had told him, as well as from overhearing the different missionaries at home. But coming from a Japanese doctor it somehow seemed to carry more weight. It was not long before he saw his life had been sinful, and recognized his need of Christ. He believed, and indicated his new faith in some poems he wrote while still in hospital.

Once well and back with his friends, however, he forgot about God. He worked conscientiously enough in his mechanical and electrical training, but had no purpose in life, and his way of living deteriorated. He developed a love for alcohol, as had his father before him, and for another six years continued to go his own way.

The Aomori church had planned a few nights of special meetings at which the speaker was to be a Pastor Shinada. He was one of the earliest Christians resulting from OMF work in Hokkaido, and had assisted the Mission in starting a small Bible School in Sapporo. Now he was its principal.

The rest of the family prayed especially that Shooji would attend these meetings, for they were getting more and more concerned about the way he was living. Although the family never nagged him, this time his father did give him a special invitation and said he hoped he would attend.

Shooji thought there would be no harm in going just to please his father. But once he was there, the words of the speaker really penetrated his heart and mind. 'How wrong it was just to accept Christ and then do nothing more about it!' he realized. 'I am truly sorry, Lord, and from now on I will follow you, whatever the cost.' He resolved that he would attend Sunday worship and the weekly prayer meeting regularly, and that when he was working he would give all the money he could save for the Lord's work.

Just at that time he had completed his course of training, and had to wait three months before beginning a new job. It seemed wise for him to get away from the influence of his former friends for a while, so Pastor Shinada suggested he should go up to Hokkaido to the Bible School for those three months. This was an unusual arrangement, but on Shinada's recommendation the School Board gave special permission. This gave Susumu much satisfaction, and the family's joy was even greater after Shooji had been up there a few weeks.

In great excitement, Umeno came to visit Michiko one day, hastily producing a letter from her bag.

'It's from Shooji,' she announced, her face beaming. 'He has written to say he feels God is telling him to stay on at the Bible School for the full course, to prepare to become a pastor!'

'How wonderful!' Michiko was as excited as her mother. 'What does Father think about it?'

'Oh, he agreed at once. He's very thankful about it, and so am I. God has been good to us.'

When she was alone again, Michiko closed her eyes. 'Thank you, Heavenly Father,' she whispered from an overflowing heart. 'This was really worth waiting for. Now there's just Ichiro's faith to continue to pray for — and Father's attitude against me. And Lord, please meet Shooji's needs, and help him to study. Guide clearly about his future, and when the time comes please find him a good Christian wife.'

Chapter Seventeen

Zion Church

SUSUMU WAS NOW ONE OF THE STRONGEST SUPPORTERS
of the Aomori Church, and Michiko continued to marvel at the way
God was using both her parents, in spite of her father's unforgiving
spirit towards her. On his retirement from the railway Susumu had
determined to serve God with his new free time, and he found plenty
of opportunities to use his commonsense and business experience; his
transformed life also bore an obvious testimony.

Often in a morning he would show up unexpectedly at the Netlands' home and say, 'Sensei, isn't there something I can do to help you
today?' He and Anton became close friends as they served the Lord
together, both in evangelistic outreach and hard manual work con-
nected with church or camp.

The Netlands and others serving on the Camp Committee had
come to the somewhat regretful conclusion that the old teahouse at
the beach near Kominato, scene of many coming to know Christ more
closely, could no longer meet the growing needs of the area. Although
additions and improvements had been made to the building periodically, times had changed. Increasing affluence was making the old
teahouse look the more dilapidated by contrast and it was also lacking
in many conveniences including warmth in winter, when snow would
sometimes blow through the cracks of the single-board structure! Nor
was it big enough to serve the growing number of Christians in Aomori
prefecture, or for the planned outreach to attract more non-Christians.

It was not only the young people such as Michiko and Tani San
who appreciated the spiritual value of the camp programs; Susumu
had come to do so. So he, with a few others among the church leaders,
felt a strong personal interest in helping to find and develop a new

camp site. With the increased prosperity, skiing had now become a very popular sport in Japan, and there were excellent skiing conditions in the nearby foothills and mountains. So the committee felt it might be best to look for a site up there, so that an all-year camping program could be set up. Property would also probably be cheaper there than in the now very popular and more crowded beach areas.

So Susumu Tamura and Oosaka San, one of the earliest converts in the Aomori work, started making enquiries about land for sale, and they would then go and survey anything which sounded possible. Susumu enjoyed these outings which reminded him a little of his old life on Karafuto, as they tramped through quiet forest land, sometimes with snow still on the ground. He and Oosaka became close friends, too, and shared their different past experiences and how they had come to Christ.

One property which sounded suitable was a five-acre tract of forest land on the foothills of eight-peaked Mt Hakoda, surrounded by more forest and farm land. Susumu and Oosaka went to view it and found it a quiet, scenic spot, yet just under an hour's drive from the city. One important feature was a spring of excellent water on the property, and it was within easy walk of good ski facilities.

With growing excitement the men returned to tell the rest of the committee about their find, and when all had seen it they were unanimous that this would best meet their need, with their limited financial resources. As soon as the land was bought the development work began. Oosaka's professional experience as a carpenter was a big help here, but Anton did much of the actual work, with the Tamuras and others giving hours of back-breaking labor to bring the dream to reality.

Once the outside structure was completed, work continued on the inside and the furnishings. The Netlands used to take their vacuum cleaner back and forth from home, and were surprised one day to see a new one out at the camp. They couldn't find where it had come from, only later learning that Susumu had seen one was needed and donated it anonymously. Both he and Umeno were most generous of their time and money for the Lord's service. Michiko, too, was greatly interested in the new camp, thinking more handicapped people could find Christ there.

The first camp was held at the new site the summer of 1967, and it can now accommodate a hundred campers. In addition to Primary, Junior-high, High School, Adult and Family camps, and College and Career Retreats, there are English Seminars both for college students and for Japanese teachers of English. A big attraction is the number of English-speaking missionaries available there, and some of the teachers have found Christ, in addition to many attending the other camps. There have been Couples' Retreats with emphasis on the Christian home; others for American personnel at the Air Base; and various Christian Workers' conferences have been held there. Since the whole area is well known for its ideal skiing conditions, in winter another opportunity to reach many with the Gospel is through ski camps. So far, only day Retreats have been arranged for the handicapped, but these have been much appreciated.

One day Anton Netland was driving along near the university when he happened to pass a student who appeared to be lame. He stopped the car and offered the student a ride to his rooming house. The young man was very impressed that a foreigner would trouble to do this, and a friendship quickly developed. Anton learned that his name was Kiyose Masuda and he was a freshman at the new university. He had had polio as a child and, though not nearly as crippled as Michiko, had been left with a slightly shuffling gait and one arm and hand partially paralysed. He was the son of a doctor who lived some distance from Aomori city, and he was determined that in spite of his handicap he would live as normal a life as possible and at least get a good education, although after that the future looked bleak and uncertain.

Kiyose accepted an invitation to the Bible study at Michiko's home, and her courageous example no doubt had a strong influence upon him. He accepted Christ and a little later, at Camp, dedicated his life for full-time service.

About the same time a nice-looking young man appeared at the Netlands' door one day and politely asked if they would teach him English. He told them his name was Terashita and he was working at a nearby hotel. He had a likeable personality, but came from a very unhappy home and was often depressed. Soon he was interested in the Bible as well as in English, and expressed a desire to believe. He too began attending the Bible studies at Michiko's home.

By this time the Kominato church was organized and independent, with its own pastor, and the new Camp (known as Aomori Christian Center, since its purpose was to serve the whole prefecture) was well established in the hands of a capable committee, and now also had a full-time resident worker named Kinichiro Miura. He was a young farmer from a country area of the prefecture who had had a very unhappy childhood. One day, however, he heard the Gospel on the Light of the World radio broadcast for which Akira Hatori was responsible and had immediately believed. He welcomed the opportunity to work at the Christian Center and could often be seen memorizing Scripture as he worked around the grounds.

So the Netlands, though still involved in the Camp program, were free to pioneer a fresh work. 'D'you know, I believe God is wanting us to start a work in the Kobata area,' Anton remarked to his wife one day. 'With these two fellows, and Michiko San and her contacts from the Colony, we would have a nice nucleus to begin with, and Miura San seems eager to try house-to-house visiting, too.'

'Yes,' Bernice agreed, 'with all the development going on there'll soon be a sizeable population there. People who've moved into a new area are often more open, too. Some in the old established villages up here are threatened with complete ostracism, aren't they, or even forced to move away if they change their religion from the particular brand of Buddhism their village has always followed.'

'Aomori's still a hard prefecture all right,' agreed Anton, 'really resistant to the Gospel. Many of those who've become Christians have come from other places, like the Tamuras. But we've seen God do miracles before, in the city and in Kominato, and we know He can again.'

Michiko already had a successful little meeting for the local children so Bernice felt it was the obvious thing to start a Sunday school nearer the center of the populated area, where there was the possibility of reaching many more children. So the Netlands arranged to begin by renting the town assembly hall each week, for Sunday school and a morning worship service. In spite of Michiko's gift for teaching children, however, she did not take the lead, feeling it was more fitting for the three young men helpers to do so, although she privately helped them prepare the lessons and visual aids. Probably, too, she was thinking of people's first reaction to the sight of a handicapped person: to come as strangers to a Christian meeting and see a crippled person directing things might make them disdain it, or withdraw in discomfort. 'It's better,' she reasoned, 'for them just to notice me in the background at first, and afterwards get to know me as a person.'

Michiko's whole heart was right behind this new venture, however. 'I'm so happy that once it's properly established there will be a church near at hand where I can encourage the handicapped to go,' she said to Anton and Bernice, 'and I could easily drive them here from the Colony.'

'It's good that your parents are really joining in here too.' Bernice said, 'even though they have been members of the Aomori church for such a long time, and have so many friends there. It's quite a journey to Kobata from their home in the city. But then, they are pioneers at heart, aren't they!'

'Susumu is a tower of strength here,' Anton agreed, 'just as he used to be over camp matters. He's eager to help in house-to-house visitation, and really enjoys talking to people and inviting them to come to the services.'

'Kiyose Masuda goes visiting with you sometimes too, doesn't he?' asked Michiko.

'Yes,' replied Anton, 'and we had a wonderful experience the other night. We went together to see that woman who's just believed, and her husband accepted Christ! They will be the first newly-converted family to be added to our embryo church.'

'Dr Masuda's very impressed with the change in his son,' Bernice added. 'Did you know, Michiko, he's twice come to thank us and others at the church for giving his son "a living hope through Jesus Christ".'

Michiko's friend and former colleague, the widowed Mi-se, and her little son occasionally visited her at her home beside the Colony, and there met Miura san who gladly attended the Bible studies when he wasn't busy at the Camp. Before long he asked Mi-se to be his wife, and adopted her son as his own. This added another Christian couple to the little group.

Gradually more and more people began to attend the services, and the Christians began to consider erecting a small building of their own, which they decided should be called Zion Church. By the time Susumu Tamura became ill, land had been secured and he had helped by approaching the neighbors about water and road access. But he never had the joy of seeing the completion of the building, nor worshipping in it.

In June 1972 Anton Netland was holding tent meetings near Tappi, on the northern peninsula. Because a 34-mile undersea tunnel to connect the islands of Honshu and Hokkaido was under construction in the area new people had moved in, many of whom probably had never heard the Gospel. Susumu, like his daughter Michiko, was now really burdened for the lost, and like her too he was out-going and talked easily to people. So he had offered to help Anton with the tent meetings. On the morning he planned to leave he didn't feel at all well, but insisted on making the two-hour journey. That afternoon a severe storm blew up. Savage winds tore the laboriously-erected tent from its moorings and they had to make hasty preparations to transfer the evening meeting to the town hall. In spite of the weather, about twenty people showed up and Susumu took part by giving testimony to his salvation, and how his life had been changed after he had formerly been a heavy drinker.

The following Sunday he attended the service in the Kominato church, in which he continued to have an interest and desire to help where he could. That was the last church service he was ever to attend. As his discomfort grew worse, cancer of the liver was diagnosed, too late for any treatment. Soon he was hospitalized and Anton saw him frequently in between the busy camp sessions. His old railway friend, Kakizaki, also visited him and at first Susumu was still able to joke with him, or else talk freely about the Gospel loudly enough so that others in the ward couldn't miss the subject of their conversation!

He rapidly grew worse, however, and when it seemed the end was near he asked Anton to arrange a communion service at the hospital. Umeno was there, of course, and Michiko and Bernice Netland, for this memorable occasion when probably for the last time this genial warrior for Christ would partake of the bread and wine. After receiving them, Susumu announced that there were some things he must say. 'First, I want to tell you, Michiko,' he said to her, 'that I forgive you for entering that prisoner's name on our family register. And I ask your forgiveness for the ill-feeling I've held against you about it. I'm sorry that I haven't always treated you very well in the past.'

He paused for a moment, then asked Anton, 'Would you do one more thing for me? It's so hot here in the hospital and I keep remembering the sweet, cold water of the spring out at the camp site. I would love to drink from it just once more.'

Anton realized it was not only the weather and the lack of air-conditioning from which Susumu was suffering, but the fever which burned his body. He set off immediately for the camp site, glad to be able to do anything to help this beloved fellow worker who had meant so much to him in recent years. As he filled a large thermos with the water he was reminded of King David's longing for a drink from the water of the well of Bethlehem (2 Sam. 23.15), and how his friends went, at great danger to themselves, to obtain it for him. How much easier his hour's drive to Moya and back, Anton thought.

On his return to the city, however, he was dismayed to find the main streets around the hospital all blocked off, and discovered the big summer festival parade was soon to pass that way. After a moment's thought, he went to find the nearest policeman and explained his errand. The policeman let him through and he thankfully walked into the hospital with his thermos bottle.

Susumu was thrilled and grateful for the water. He knew he had not much longer to live, and in his weak voice begged Anton and the others present, 'You will look after my wife, won't you?' 'Of course', they promised.

An adult camp was scheduled for the following week, but on the morning it started, Sunday August 13, the phone rang at the camp site and Anton was told that Susumu Tamura was dying. He hurried back to the city and reached the hospital just in time to be beside his friend as he went into the presence of his Lord. Umeno and their eldest son, Ichiro, were with him too.

It seemed most appropriate to hold the funeral service at the camp which Susumu had done so much to bring into being, and which he had worked for so lovingly and faithfully. So it was arranged for the following Wednesday afternoon, so that campers who wished to do so could stay on for it after the camp program concluded at noon.

On the two evenings before a funeral in Japan, it is customary to hold a kind of wake, or open house for friends and neighbors to come and view the body in his home. Naturally all the Christians wanted some Christian witness to be included and it made a difficult and rather hectic time for the Netlands, Pastor and Mrs Kamata and some of the elders, having to care for all these arrangements and at the same time carry on with the Camp program. Yet there was increased blessing at the camp as many were touched by the news of Susumu's death; it brought the reality of heaven closer to all.

The body was cremated in the morning, so there was no coffin at the service for anyone to come and 'worship' at, nor was there need for pall bearers. Ichiro carried in the small box of bones and ashes, covered with a purple cloth, and placed it in front of the camp auditorium which was packed with people. In addition to the campers, many of Susumu's former fellow-workers on the railway were present, and other non-Christian friends, as well as representatives from various churches in the prefecture who had come to do him honor.

Although Susumu Tamura's death was a very real and painful loss to all his friends and loved ones, and to the churches he had strengthened so markedly with his presence, yet the service sounded a note of triumph. Here, as at his mother's funeral, the congregation had not come to mourn like those who have no hope, but rather to rejoice with one who had just passed into the presence of his loving Lord.

For Michiko it was an especially poignant time. Throughout the first twenty years of her life her feelings for her father had been largely negative. She had realized later, however, that perhaps much of his behavior stemmed from being an adopted son, and that only after the death of her grandparents had he been able to assert himself as a capable and caring head of his family.

Those had been happy years when he first became a Christian, and then had backed her in her new project of building the House of Grace; then had come his long-burning anger at what he considered her outrageous conduct in adding a prisoner's name to their family record.

'That's almost fourteen years ago now', she reflected, 'and it hasn't had the slightest adverse effect on the family — or it least it wouldn't have had if father hadn't obstinately let it cloud our relationship all these years. He was stubborn all right — just like me,' she had to admit ruefully, 'we really were a lot alike. How thankful I am that he apologized and asked for my forgiveness before he died.'

The thought of Taikichi's name on the family register reminded Michiko that it was about time to visit him again. It wasn't so easy now that she was an employee at the busy Colony, and with Riyoko not there to help. But she must make arrangements as soon as the summer holiday crowds had lessened on the trains. At least it would be nice to go this time knowing her father had overcome his hostility at last.

After Susumu's death, Umeno stayed on in the family home with Ichiro, the eldest son, and his family. She felt she should continue to support the new work at Zion Church which her husband had been so interested in, and gave liberally of her time and counsel. Her business experience in Karafuto, her strength of character deepened through the many hardships she had experienced there and since — the loss of material things, three children and now her husband — together with her strong faith in Christ and her cheerful patience, all fitted her well to counsel others facing a wide variety of problems.

'Material and labor costs are rising rapidly', Anton said as they discussed things one day. 'I think the wisest thing would be to erect the outside frame of the church as soon as possible, then we can work on the inside during the winter months, as funds allow'. So the little group of Christians agreed to get an estimate from Mr Oosaka. They found that in addition to the comparatively small sum already on hand, about $1,300 would be needed to do the very minimum to close the building before winter. To the missionaries this seemed an insuperable obstacle, but Michiko and her mother were undeterred.

'Don't you worry about this, Sensei,' Umeno Tamura said to Anton. 'We're going to have another meeting to pray and talk about it.'

They arranged this a few days later, and didn't even tell the missionaries. Next day a beaming Umeno came to see them.

'Sensei, it's all taken care of. We have the money,' she said. 'Isn't God good!' The Netlands never did hear where it all came from.

Soon carpenters were busy on the site, and were able to close the framework of the new Zion Church that fall. Anton and Miura San worked on the inside throughout the winter, and even while this was still in progress they were able to begin using the building as a meeting place.

There was to be a crowning joy in Zion Church, however, which none of the Tamura family could have foreseen when they first began to assist in the work.

One place where the OMF had opened work in Hokkaido was the mining town of Mikasa. The first missionaries found there a fairly elderly couple named Kudoo, who had become Christians years before through a Holiness pastor they had met and who had remained true to the Lord although there was no church in Mikasa then. Later, Lorna Edwards went to carry on the work there, and at that time the Kudoo family opened their home for a Sunday night Bible study. The youngest of their three daughters, Miyako, was in Junior High School then, and always attended the meetings, seeming really hungry to know God's Word.

Eventually Miyako went away to train as a teacher. She wanted to serve the Lord as best she could, and characteristically decided to become a teacher at a school for handicapped children — a job that would have had no appeal for most Japanese then. Lorna kept up the friendship with Miyako when she came home on her days off, and later when Lorna was teaching at the Bible School in Sapporo Miyako would occasionally spend a night with her there, or they would meet at conferences for all Hokkaido Christians.

Once Lorna met her just a few months after the new, modern translation of the Japanese Bible had been published, and was surprised to see Miyako's copy was already worn black around the edges.

'How did you get it so black and worn-looking already?' Lorna asked.

'Oh, I just want to read this new version right through as quickly as possible to find all the treasures in it!' Miyako explained with a smile. 'So I always carry it, and open it in all kinds of places.'

Lorna was at the Bible School during Shooji Tamura's first year there, but the following year went temporarily to take charge of the work at the nearest port city of Otaru. And who should be sent from the Bible School to assist there on Sundays but Shooji Tamura!

Lorna noticed that his new version Bible looked well used, too, and got blacker and blacker around the edges Sunday by Sunday as he held it to speak to the Sunday School children, or to take part in the worship service. In fact, it became quite a topic of conversation among the church people, and when Lorna accidentally spilt hot water into his briefcase one Sunday as they all ate the noon meal together at the church, that didn't improve its appearance! So when Christmas came and they all wanted to show their appreciation for his help, the church members presented Shooji with a beautiful new Bible.

When Shooji had completed his training at the Bible School in Sapporo he went to assist the pastor at a TEAM church in the city of Yokosuka, a big naval base near Tokyo. This was not only valuable experience in church work, but it also gave him the opportunity to become familiar with the Japanese church organization known as the Domei, to which most churches begun by TEAM missionaries are affiliated. But before he went to Yokosuka, Shooji and Miyako had got to know one another, through Miyako's best friend marrying Terashita San who had been one of the initial group starting Zion church, and who was a friend of Shooji's.

To the great joy of everyone who knew them both, these two young people, each with a Bible so quickly worn with use, became engaged and were married in the Aomori church's beautiful new building in September 1975. Many friends from both Hokkaido and Aomori gathered for the occasion. Characteristic of these two young people who had so clearly demonstrated their love for the Bible in the past were the first words on the printed program of their wedding ceremony: 'The grass withers, the flower fades; but the *Word of our God* will stand for ever.' (Isaiah 40.8)

Anton and Miura San had been working steadily, all through the winter and beyond, on the interior of the little Zion Church building, and now it was finished. In addition to the auditorium and a Sunday school room downstairs, there was an upstairs apartment for a pastor. And shortly before the wedding the Netlands had had to move down to Tokyo. So it came about that the church issued a call to Shooji, and after their marriage the young couple were able to move into this new apartment and begin a helpful ministry there.

Normally it might not be easy for a young man to pastor a small church where his mother and elder sister were members, and were also Christians of much longer standing than himself. There can be dangers, too, in one family having too strong an influence in a church. But Umeno Tamura is a very wise and gentle person, in spite of her depth of character, and Shooji seems to be handling things well.

With her teacher's training and experience with handicapped children, his wife Miyako has been a great help in the church too. On the Sunday morning when I was present there seemed to be a flourishing Sunday school of about 40-50 children, with Michiko teaching the youngest group. There were about 20 adults at the service, and it was a particularly joyous occasion because Terashita and his wife were being farewelled before leaving to work in a Christian bookstore in Hokkaido.

Four in the congregation that morning were handicapped and so Michiko is seeing fulfilled her desire for some from the Colony to come to a knowledge of Christ as Savior, and then becoming fully accepted members of the church. One girl from the Colony had always had the dream that one day she would go to Hawaii, the most wonderful place she had ever heard of. But when she found new life in Christ, she told Umeno Tamura on the day of her baptism, 'I don't need to go to Hawaii now. I'm going to Heaven, which is far more wonderful.' Other Christians at the Colony attend the Aomori church, with which they have had a longer connection.

Through the new Zion Church Michiko has gained something else of great value: in the pastor's wife she has a new sister and a very understanding friend of the handicapped. Shooji now leads the Bible study in Michiko's house, and to their great joy their elder brother, Ichiro, sometimes attends. So they look forward to the day when their whole family will be one in Christ.

Chapter Eighteen

With God All Things are Possible

MICHIKO WAS SITTING AT HOME one day feeling unusually 'flat' and weary. Perhaps it was because there was no immediate challenge to tackle just now: things were going well at the church, with her brother installed as pastor, and the Colony was certainly a going concern. Yet her many duties could be frustrating at times, and even with her greatly improved mobility thanks to the car and to good leg braces, she sometimes felt terribly tired physically, and mentally too through the constant need of counselling her charges.

She still felt lonely at times too in spite of the many people surrounding her at the Colony. She had never quite got over the loss of her two former great friends. It had been so nice to see more of Mi-se in recent years since she had been married to Miura San — she had frequently enjoyed their company in her home. But now he had felt called to the ministry, and they had left for a Bible School in western Japan where he was training to be a pastor. Michiko was very happy for her and this wonderful opportunity of service, and for Riyoko too happily married to a Christian husband. Not so long ago it would have been unthinkable for girls in their condition to have anyone willing to arrange a marriage for them, even though they were not so crippled as Michiko. 'What a difference Christianity has made,' she reflected, 'and of course I do rejoice for them. But I can't help feeling a little lonely.'

The morning mail arrived, and Michiko listlessly sorted out the business things and found only one personal letter. She was glad to see that it was from Pastor Uetaki, and she quickly opened it, thinking as she did so that he would certainly have an encouraging word from the Lord for her.

As she unfolded the letter and began to read, the rest of her body suddenly felt as limp as her useless legs. She hastily skipped through the formal greetings again, and stopped at the second paragraph.

'I have just heard from the prison officials,' the pastor had written, 'that in view of his long record of good behavior and evidence of reformed character, your husband has been recommended for clemency and an early release from prison......'

The letter fell on the table as Michiko's normally powerful fingers began to tremble, and it seemed as if the room was spinning round before her eyes. She feared for a moment that she was going to faint.

It was so totally unexpected! Though Taikichi was no longer an inmate of death row, his sentence was still life imprisonment in spite of his family's many appeals, and they had all expected this to be literally fulfilled.

'But when I added his name to the family record at the ward office, before I even met him, that was just a technical convenience,' she thought dazedly. 'I felt compassion for a fellow human being who was thought to be close to death, and so evidently in need of Christ.'

After her visit, and the later change in his sentence, she had been embarrassed one day to receive word from a Buddhist priest in the prefecture, saying he was the government appointed social worker to ensure the welfare of the prisoners' relatives, and was there anything he could do for her? Michiko had hastily written back to assure him she was self-supporting and had no particular needs at present, but would let him know should any arise.

From the legal point of view, of course, the name could as easily be removed from the family record as it had been placed there, given the necessary signatures. But was that what she really wanted?

As the sudden, dizzying prospect of a husband to share her home hit her, after almost a lifetime of assurances that such a thing would always be impossible, a strange warmth began to suffuse Michiko's numbed senses. Through her visits over the years she had come to have a real regard and respect for Taikichi, and believed him innocent.

'Though I've never envisaged living with him.....'

But why not?

The difficulties marshalled themselves in her mind with overwhelming force. Where could they live? He would probably never be accepted in his own community — such a thing was almost impossible for someone with a criminal record in Japan. And the same would be true here ..... and what about the family's horror and disapproval?

The thought surged through her mind like a roaring wave bent on destroying all before it. 'What recriminations there will be from mother and my brothers! How could I ever have done such a mad and disgraceful thing to the family record?

'And what about Taikichi? Once he's free, he may have second thoughts about being tied to a cripple for the rest of his life. People have always told me that no one would want that...... On the other hand, it's not very likely that any family would be willing to arrange a marriage for their daughter with a supposed murderer.....'

Anyone else would probably have been pacing the floor by this time, but that form of release was impossible for Michiko. Instead she just pressed the tips of her strong, sensitive fingers tightly together while all these thoughts went racing through her mind. At last she remembered to pray, and finally realized she had not finished reading the letter. It stated that since Taikichi had been in prison for twenty years, and the usual problems of adapting to normal society would be intensified by coming to such a cold climate as Aomori after life in the warm south, the pastor thought she probably should not expect him before the spring.

Michiko let out a slow sigh of relief. The winter was not yet far advanced, so there would be time to think, and above all pray. Here was certainly a towering wall it would be impossible to leap in her own strength. The more she thought about it, the more complicated and unbelievable the matter seemed. She found herself experiencing a strange mixture of ill-defined fear, and a faint glow of satisfaction. Yet she hadn't the slightest idea whether Taikichi would wish to continue their relationship; and after being independent so long, would she herself, with her strong will, be willing or able to adapt to the role of a submissive Japanese wife?

After a few days of earnest prayer about the matter, Michiko felt assured that if Taikichi was willing, then she would take this as the culmination of God's perfect will for her.

Soon a letter arrived from the prison officials asking what she would be able to do to help her husband adjust to civilian life if he were released. So it seemed that he must have indicated his willingness to continue as her husband, and she must now produce some concrete proposals for finding him work. For this she would need help, and she realized she could not put off much longer the dreaded task of breaking the news to her family. She had written to Pastor Uetaki asking his advice, however, and thought she would wait for his reply first.

It came quickly, saying that whatever might have happened in the past, judging by what he had witnessed of the change in Taikichi over the years he believed Michiko need have no undue fears about the future. Of course there were always many adjustments to make in every marriage, and these might not be easy, but they could count on God's help. He also suggested that he should conduct the Christian marriage ceremony at his own church, as soon as Taikichi was released, thus saving Michiko and her family embarrassment up in their own area.

With this encouragement and answer to her prayers for guidance, Michiko now braced herself to tackle the remaining wall of expected opposition from her family. She had decided, after much thought, that Shooji would probably be the best one to approach first. After all, he was a pastor and had more experience of the world and the need of counsel in various situations. Then perhaps he could help her break the news to her mother. So she phoned Shooji to ask if she could see him alone.

'I don't think Father or Mother ever talked to you about Taikichi, my husband, did they?' she began.

'Your *what*?' Shooji looked as if he was afraid she had taken leave of her senses.

So she had to begin at the beginning and tell him the whole story, while Shooji registered utter astonishment.

'No wonder Father was so angry! You certainly have lived an eventful life, and caused us many surprises, Michiko,' he said when she had finished. 'But I do believe God is in this. My wife and I will certainly go down with you for the wedding, and give you all the support we can.'

Michiko expressed her profound gratitude, and added, 'Do pray about Mother's reaction, too.'

'Yes, that may be quite a problem. But with God all things are possible, remember. Perhaps it will help if we tell her together.'

So they went to find Umeno. It was unusual for her to see her two very busy children together, and after the polite preliminary greetings she probably was not surprised when Michiko said she had some important news. But even that did not help to prepare her for the shock of what she heard.

'You remember Taikichi, who is registered on our family record as my husband,' Michiko began. 'I've heard from the prison that he is to be released soon.'

Umeno's usually sweet face was suddenly contorted with more rage and fear than Michiko could remember seeing even in their most terrible experiences back in Karafuto.

'Why would the government let such a person loose on society?' she stormed. 'What are they thinking about? It's absolutely disgraceful!'

'But it's because his conduct has been consistently good for the whole twenty years he has been there,' Shooji answered gently. 'Society is becoming more humane now, remember, and in any case there has never been real proof he was guilty.'

Umeno appeared entirely unconvinced. 'But how can we *know*? And anyone who has been in prison can never come to any good! Why, *why* did you ever do such a wicked, stupid thing?' she added, turning to Michiko. 'You've brought nothing but trouble and disgrace to the family with your stubborn self-will. Whatever would your father say now?'

Michiko couldn't help feeling thankful he was not there, and explained once again that the prisoner had been near execution, and that was the only way to see him and tell him about Christ.

'But once he believed, there was no need for you to go on seeing him! There's this pastor down there. He can take care of him. You must have his name removed from the record at once!'

Michiko drew a deep breath. 'But I really like him, Mother. He's a gentle kind of person, with a good record for his work in prison, as well as his character.'

Umeno looked at her with undisguised horror, and Shooji hastily intervened.

'Don't be afraid, Mother. I know what a great shock this must be to you, but we really believe God is behind it and we will pray that you, too, will come to see it that way.'

Their prayers were answered. As Umeno herself prayed too, the Holy Spirit gradually worked in her heart and miraculously enabled her to overcome age-old natural prejudices, and to accept that God had done a work of grace in a prisoner's life, as He had done in those of her own family. Before long she actually found herself looking forward to meeting Taikichi!

So Michiko had the joy of being supported by her family as she informed the church elders, and she was able to tell the probation officer that they would be responsible for finding work for Taikichi in Aomori.

Possibly as a result of this, near the end of January they suddenly got word that Taikichi was to be released in ten days time, much earlier than previously suggested. Hurried arrangements had to be

made for the wedding, and then one bureaucratic regulation threatened to spoil everything. It could even have cast a faint fear in Michiko's
mind as to whether she would see her husband again!

Taikichi's home, where his mother lay bed-ridden, was in the
southermost island of Japan. Naturally she was most anxious to see
him after the long separation, and the city where the prison and Pastor
Uetaki's church were situated was much nearer to her home than to
Aomori. Yet regulations required that Taikichi must first report to the
probation officer in Aomori before he could visit his mother. This
would naturally involve a very long and expensive double journey.

Another problem was to find work for Taikichi. At first Michiko
had hoped he could help out at the Camp, since there was always
maintenance to be done there. But the Netlands had left the area, so
that posed a problem. Then Umeno thought of her husband's old
friend, Oosaka San, in the city. Perhaps he could do with another
worker, since Taikichi had become a fine cabinet maker. Michiko's
home would be rather a long way from some of his jobs, but Oosaka
San was willing to take him on, so that problem was happily settled.

The day came for Michiko once again to set out on the long,
tiring journey south. But how different were the circumstances this
time! Now she was supported by her mother, and Shooji and his wife,
and instead of heading for the grim interior of a prison she was on her
way to a Christian church as a bride, a role for which, humanly
speaking, it had seemed she could never be destined.

The pastor had arranged that Taikichi should come straight from
the prison to the church to be baptized, and the wedding ceremony
was to be two hours later, since he must report in Aomori as soon as
possible.

As soon as Umeno saw Taikichi she loved him, and her heart was
really at peace. His brothers and sisters came, glad of the opportunity
to be reunited after twenty years, and were no doubt amazed to be at a
wedding for which their family had been spared all the details, since
the pastor himself had undertaken all the responsibilities of the go-
between.

In his address, the pastor stressed that before God all men are
sinners, and all need to confess and repent. For twenty years now,
however, Taikichi had kept the law in prison, and was now beginning a
new life with God's help. He then went on to emphasize the need for
mutual love and concern, and for holiness of character.

It was a short and simple ceremony, yet so strange were all the
circumstances which had led up to it that to those present who knew

the backgrounds of the two participants, this marriage indeed bore evidence of having been planned in heaven. With full hearts and with a deeper understanding of its meaning, they joined in the singing of the final hymn of praise.

> Praise, my soul, the King of heaven,
> To His feet thy tribute bring;
> Ransomed, healed, restored, forgiven,
> Who like thee His praise should sing?
> Praise Him! Praise Him! Praise Him! Praise Him!
> Praise the everlasting King.
>
> Father-like He tends and spares us;
> Well our feeble frame He knows;
> In His hands He gently bears us,
> Rescues us from all our foes.
> Praise Him! Praise Him! Praise Him! Praise Him!
> Widely as His mercy flows.
>
> Angels, help us to adore Him;
> Ye behold Him face to face;
> Sun and moon bow down before Him,
> Dwellers all in time and space.
> Praise Him! Praise Him! Praise Him! Praise Him!
> Praise with us the God of grace.

Based on Psalm 103   Henry Francis Lyte (1793 - 1847)

Postscript

IT WAS MY LAST FULL DAY IN AOMORI, and I had just spent half an hour at Umeno Tamura's home, looking at old pictures of Karafuto. When we mentioned we were going to take a look at Hamango, Umeno eagerly offered to show us the area. Since her husband's death she had not travelled about much, and in fact had not been to Hamango for a number of years, so she welcomed the opportunity to do so now.

As we neared Kominato she was surprised at first that she could not find the way to the little hamlet. At last, on enquiry, we were directed to an overgrown dirt road which seemed headed in the direction of the little branch railway line from Kominato, its track now almost lost to sight in weeds. As we finally bumped over the level crossing, Umeno gasped in astonishment.

Before us was a wide, circular area covered with ragged grass, bamboo and other shrubs growing to a height of four feet or more. Just here and there we could see a few bits of wood and brick, all that remained of the foundations of the former buildings.

Dazedly Umeno sought to get her bearings from the position of the railway track.

'That's where our house was,' she exclaimed at last, pointing excitedly, 'but — everything's gone!'

Indeed it had. What had been built from poor materials in wartime extremity was no longer required, and all the former residents had long since moved to better houses in burgeoning Aomori, or Kominato, anything at all usable having been salvaged. The rest of the old buildings had collapsed among the weeds.

Nostalgia gripped Umeno for a moment as she thought back to

the hardships of those old days. Yet it was here that Michiko had first told them she had become a Christian. It was here that Allen Fadel had come with the Gospel and she herself had believed. Here God had enabled them to leap over another difficult wall — the intense pressure in the village to conform and to continue ancestor worship. Yes, the old life was behind them now. How good God had been to them!

From there she took us to see the old family home in Kominato, which had been replaced by a beautiful new house, and the new Kominato church building. During the forty-minute ride back to Aomori she reminisced about a number of things, and it was then she told us about Michiko learning to drive.

Soon she came to the present, however. It was sixteen months now since Michiko's wedding, and her mother mentioned that she had only recently returned from spending a few weeks with them in the house near the Colony. Michiko had had a very busy schedule just then, and her husband was working on a job some distance away, so Umeno had gone over there to help. Among other things she had been getting up very early to make the *danna-sama's* lunch, ready for him to take when he left for work at 5.30 am. Those of us listening, hearing the term of respect used for her daughter's husband and seeing the contented smile on her face, realized there was no doubt at all that Umeno was very pleased with her new son-in-law.

During our last visit with Michiko, she indicated that she probably would soon not need to be employed as a teacher — implying with a shy twinkle in her eyes that her husband would be in a position to support her.

More recent news still is that Taikichi is established in his own business, and Michiko has resigned from her paid employment at the Colony. A few months of physical and mental rest have now given her the opportunity to perceive a new vision of need. She believes God would have her bring into being a fifty-bed home for people too crippled to be able to work in the Colony, and that it should be a wholly Christian-run institution. The city authorities have given initial approval, but there remains plenty of red tape to unsnarl or hurdle, and support to raise, before building can start. Michiko is learning patience, however, and for her this is just another wall to leap in God's time and strength.

Appendix 1

The Meiji Restoration

For 200 years before 1868, the Japanese had been completely cut off from the outside world by their military rulers, the Tokugawa Shogunate. The only exception had been a very limited trade with the Dutch and Chinese at one or two specified ports. No Japanese had been allowed abroad, and ocean-going ships had ceased to be built. The hereditary Emperors were confined to the ancient city of Kyoto with largely religious and cultural court functions to perform, while the Tokugawas ruled from Edo (now Tokyo), determined to preserve the country from any contact with suspect Roman Catholic missionaries and traders from the west.

Finally, however, Commodore Perry of the United States Navy appeared off the coast near Edo with his ominous 'black ships' and forced the Shogunate regime to open up some ports to the western nations for the supplying of their ships, and the beginning of international trade.

Amid internal confusion and unrest, the Imperial line was restored to power and a new Constitution written which provided freedom of speech, writing, worship, and the right of a subject to reside where he pleased. It was this which had brought the Tamura family to their new property in Aomori, and which now made a choice possible for the sons. The new Constitution also declared the Emperor to be divine and inviolable and invested him with legislative powers with the consent of the Diet or Parliament.

Appendix 2

Brief History of Sakhalin prior to this story

1264	A Chinese expedition to the island was resisted by the Ainu.
1287	A Chinese garrison was stationed there.
1409	Reports of a Chinese traveller, Hsing Shu, visiting the island.
1630s	The Ming dynasty was gradually pushed out of the lower Amur region by the growing power of the Manchu, whose long-lasting dynasty continued to 1917.
1635	A Japanese expedition to the island, known to them as Karafuto ('place where the Chinese people are').
1643	The first European known to visit the island was a Dutchman, Capt. Vries, who was sent from the Dutch East Indies to look for a legendary island 'rich in gold and silver.'
1644	China records receiving tribute from Tungus, Gilyak and Ainu in the Amur region, and probably from those on Sakhalin as well.
1645	A Russian, Pojarkov, descended the Amur and heard reports of a large island at its mouth, and of people called Gilyaks, 'who keep in their villages five hundred to a thousand dogs, and train bears to do peaceful work.'
1649	The Japanese map the island.
1689	China and Russia signed the treaty of Nerchursk, which excluded the Russians from the Amur region. Instead, they concentrated on the North Kurile Islands. Not until 1805 is another Russian known to have been on the island. Between these two dates individual Cossacks may have ventured there, but no reliable record of this exists. Russians have later claimed the furs the Cossacks were looking for were *tribute* collected from Gilyaks, and therefore Russia had the original sovereignty over the island.
1700	Sakhalin's Ainu, Gilyak and Oroki sent tribute missions to Manchu ports and developed trade. They exchanged valuable furs for brocade, beads, fans, pipes and needles, and later exchanged these

with Japanese merchants who had begun to visit the south of the island. Tribute to the Manchu continued until 1820.

1709   Chinese Emperor K'ang Shi engaged three French Jesuit priests to map his territory in the east as far as the coast of Tartary. These men were able to consult the map already made by the Japanese. When sending copies of their maps back to France they wrote across the mouth of the Amur river, 'Saghalien oula anga hata', the local equivalent of 'the cliffs of the black river', probably referring to a cape at the river mouth. In France the writing was mistakenly thought to be the name of the large island near the river mouth, and copies simply put 'Saghalien' which was subsequently Russianized to 'Sakhalin'.

1790   The Japanese government constructed guard posts on the south coast of the island, and set up a permanent trade center. Exploration and economic development also increased in Hokkaido, and the Southern Kuriles. The industrial revolution was in full progress in the west, and many foreign ships were now coming to the Pacific. Russia had now seized all the Tartary coast, calling it her Maritime Province. This was only 25 miles from Hokkaido and south Sakhalin, and Japan for the first time felt the threat of a western foreign power on her borders.

1805   Former Russian contact with Sakhalin had been on its north-west coast. Now a Capt. Krusenstern surveyed the south coast, and was impressed with its potential as a depot for opening trade with Japan, Korea and China. On his return he proposed his government should seize that area, since he considered Japan too weak to resist. He conceded it could be considered unjust, but rationalized that if Russia didn't do it, some other European power would. It would then be easy for them to attack Russia through Siberia. His government waited nearly fifty years to follow his advice.

1806   In October the Russians and Japanese clashed for the first time on Sakhalin. A Lt. Khvostov with a friend raided and burned Japanese settlements in the south, around Aniwa Bay. Their government had not ordered this; it was rather the result of personal frustration after six months of fruitless attempt to reach a trade agreement with Japan, as all Western nations were then trying to do. The Russians burned all the boats in Aniwa Bay, so news of the attack only reached the Japanese mainland the next summer.

1807   The news caused rage and alarm throughout the country, and the Shogun government claimed the whole island as Japanese territory.

1811   In retaliation for Lt. Khvostov's action, Japan captured a Russian survey team.

1813   Russia finally apologized for the attack on Aniwa Bay. Soviet historians later put a different interpretation on the incident, saying

Khvostov's mission was peaceful until the Japanese started shooting. They were 'patriots' reclaiming Russian land illegally seized by Japan. They claim Khvostov raised the Russian flag on Sakhalin, thus sealing the island's ownership. Forty years of peace followed. The Japanese military on Hokkaido lost interest, and withdrew the garrisons from Karafuto, all contacts with the island being by private merchants and fishermen. The Russians, too, lost interest, directing their attention to Alaska and problems in Europe.

1846   The Japanese government sponsored an exploration trip on the island. The Russian Foreign Minister, after having for some years ordered Sakhalin to be left untouched to avoid confrontation with the Japanese, now declared the question of Russian interest there closed for ever.

1849   The Russian Governor General of their eastern provinces realized Japan was now weak from internal disorder and the tottering Shogunate was being pressured by foreign powers to open Japanese ports. On receiving his report, Tsar Nicholas I, after some hesitation — for it was still officially Chinese territory — sanctioned a circumspect exploration of the lower Amur region. The leader of this went beyond his commission, flew the Russian flag, and told the natives there that they were henceforth subjects of the Tsar. This same man, after seeing a Gilyak from Sakhalin wearing a piece of coal as a button, sent a survey team to look for coal deposits. When two were discovered on the west coast, a second mission followed to find suitable places for Russian settlements, and to inform any English, American or Japanese that Sakhalin was Russian territory.

1853   In August the first Russian settlement was established on the west coast at the 50th Parallel, ostensibly because they feared U.S. Commodore Perry or the British might attempt to land there. In October a second settlement and fort were established in the south in Aniwa Bay, right alongside the Japanese already settled there. The Russians told them they were occupying Sakhalin to defend it from the Americans. Naturally there were tensions between these two groups.

1854   In May the Russian garrisons were suddenly evacuated because of new circumstances. A Russian Admiral was visiting Japan, still trying to get a trade agreement with its government, and didn't want to scare them over Sakhalin. Also the Crimean war broke out in Europe, between Russia, and France and Britain.

1856   The Treaty of Shimoda was signed which ambiguously declared Sakhalin 'A joint possession of Russia and Japan', but Japan was recognized as owning the Southern Kuriles.

1858   Russia pressured a weakening China to sign a treaty which gave them the left bank of the Amur, in fact meaning control of that huge area. Sakhalin was not mentioned, but Russia 'assumed' that to be included. Now they felt they could tackle Japan with its falling Shogunate.

1859   The Governor General of Siberia arrived in Tokyo with an agreement whose terms stated Sakhalin was a Russian territory, but that the Japanese might freely travel and fish there. Japan naturally refused to sign it. As internal conflicts continued, however, and the Meiji Restoration was accomplished, opinions in Japan began to be divided about Karafuto, some thinking it a dangerous liability. They had already spent a lot on it, with little return. The climate was bad and they were now turning their attention to Korea and Formosa which seemed more suitable for colonization.

1875   In May, Japan signed the Treaty of St Petersburg in which they agreed to exchange Japanese rights to Sakhalin, where they had had associations for two hundred years, for all the Kurile Islands. They retained important privileges on Sakhalin, however: a consular office in their main center in the south; compensation for immovable property; and their vessels would have duty-free access to that port for ten years. Japanese fishermen could continue operations, while residents could retain their nationality and right to continue industries, and would be exempt from taxation for life. Thus the expensive and explosive border issue was defused, and Japan gained three decades for internal consolidation and economic development, but never forgot her emotional and economic ties with Karafuto.

1875 - 1905 has been termed Sakhalin's Dark Ages, when the island stagnated as a vast Russian penal colony, with all kinds of horrors suffered by both convicts and free settlers. Coal miners ate tallow candles and rotten wood while rivers were clogged with salmon. Though the coal was of high quality, carelessness and inadequate drainage spoilt the deposts and the inertia and insensitivity of the bureaucracy degraded Sakhalin to world-wide disrepute. Convicts and exiles swelled the Russian population from three thousand to 35,000, but there was no practical plan of colonization. With the sudden influx of foreigners, too, the tribespeople contracted smallpox, measles and syphilis, as well as many being murdered by escaped convicts.

1904   Meanwhile the Japanese had not neglected their privileges in the south, and their numbers grew to seven thousand. Attracted by the island's notoriety and mystery, scientists, scholars, journalists and assorted world travellers had made their way to it in the last decade, either travelling across Europe on the new Trans-Siberian Railway or up from Japan. Geologists uncovered more of its natural wealth, ethnographers studied the tribespeople, and writers exposed the evil of the penal system. Russia became alarmed. First she reneged on some provisions of the St Petersburg treaty, saying Japanese fishing rights had to be renewed annually, and she closed half their ports. The Japanese government retaliated by threatening the source of Russia's tax income. In February the legal bickering broke into war-fare.

1905   The Russo-Japanese war ended in September with dramatic naval and military victories for the Japanese which astounded western ob-servers, and caused them to re-evaluate this Asian nation. The Japanese quickly noted that military might brought greater respect than all their other efforts at modernization, including their ex-cellent universal education system which was in advance of Britain's.

The result of the war altered the balance of power in north east Asia, checking Russia's economic and political designs on Korea and Manchuria, and increasing Japan's involvement there. In fact it was the clash of interests there, rather than on Sakhalin, which pre-cipitated the war. The Japanese attack on the Russians in the north of the island was hardly noticed by the rest of the world, but was actually the only Russian territory invaded, and so perpetuated the rivalry of the two nations there. From Russia's point of view the attack was 'a cynical opportunist piece of territorial brigandage', and a later Soviet historian hints it was urged by America and Britain. But the Japanese were eager to avenge the 'humiliation' of 1875, and needed no prodding from outside.

Japan naturally assumed the whole island was now theirs, but a shock awaited them when the two sides met in the United States to draw up the Treaty of Portsmouth. The Russian delegate absolutely refused to give up their part of Sakhalin, or pay an indemnity for war expenses. Since both sides were financially exhausted by the war Theodore Roosevelt persuaded the Japanese to settle for less. The final terms partitioned Sakhalin at the 50th Parallel, the southern half, henceforth to be called Karafuto, belonging to Japan. Bitter disillusionment followed at home, where the 50th Parallel now symbolized a national shame to those who had dreamed of re-covering the whole island.

A similar feeling was expressed by Russian patriots, of course, who were left with the slightly larger but colder and less fertile north, though it had most of the coal and newly-discovered oil fields. At first they made great efforts to develop it, but couldn't get free settlers, 'since all over Russia the word "Sakhalin" was a synonym for a living hell.'

1914   When war broke out in Europe, however, and it was announced that the inhabitants of Sakhalin would be exempt from military service, over 15,000 would-be settlers rushed across Siberia to the island.

1920   Taking advantage of Russia's preoccupation first with the war, then its revolution, and the struggle between the White Russians and red Bolsheviks in Sakhalin, Japan invaded the north, claiming it as retaliation for the Bolshevik killing of seven hundred Japanese settlers on the Asian mainland. Japan continued to hold the whole island for five years. The reasons for this were fear of Bolshevism and of north Sakhalin becoming a base to attack Japan; the need for oil on which they were dependent for both naval and industrial needs; and above all the conviction that the island really was part of Japan.

1924   The Soviet regime was now firmly established at home, and recognized abroad. Anti-Japanese immigration laws in the U.S. provoked a reaction at home which pushed Japan towards international isolation. A Sino-Soviet Treaty of Friendship in this year aroused concern that Japan's special interests in China might be jeopardized. She was also feeling the need to establish diplomatic relations with the USSR for economic reasons.

1925   So in January Japan and the Soviets met at the Peking Convention at which Japan reluctantly gave up claim to north Sakhalin, withdrawing her military forces but retaining, for the next 45 years, rights to exploit minerals, forests and other natural resources there, especially coal and oil.

Appendix 3

The tribes of Sakhalin

The Oroki were one of three primitive tribes on Sakhalin, the others being the Ainu and Gilyak. Anthropologists think the Ainu settled there first, probably coming from Japan, but they themselves have a tradition of finding pit-dwelling people there before them, who made vessels of clay. The Ainu were followed by the more numerous Gilyak who appear to be a semi-Mongolian, semi-Tungus race, having language links with North Pacific Asians and Americans, and with features very similar to North American Indians.

The Oroki probably followed the Gilyak to Sakhalin about three centuries ago, and also appear to be part Tungus (of whom the Manchu are the most distinguished branch) through inter-marriage with other tribes on the Tartar mainland. The first mention of them in western records was by three Jesuit Fathers sent by the Chinese Emperor in 1709 to map the far outposts of his empire. These men penetrated to the lower reaches of the great Amur whose mouth is guarded by the northern section of Sakhalin. The Chinese had named the Oroki the 'Fish skin people' since they were clothed in dried salmon skins, and from 1700-1820 the Oroki, Ainu and Gilyak had all sent tribute to the Emperor from Sakhalin.

In 1895 at least 750 Oroki were reported on the island, but by the time of Michiko's sickness possibly 600 remained. Their own tradition said the Oroki had sprung from a male and female birch tree, and they had no record of ever having a great king or chief. Yet they appeared more intelligent than the other tribes, and many could speak Gilyak as well as their own language. They were also superior hunters and traders.

The name Oro or Oron in Manchu means reindeer, of which these people had large herds to draw their sleds, loaded with valuable furs, to the mainland in winter. The Gilyaks only used dog sleds. The Oroki lived in portable skin tents in the forests in the long winter months, and hunted. In summer they moved to wood huts near rivers and the coast, to take advantage of the abundant supplies of fish, especially salmon. Thus it was that Michiko and the groups of sick people were able to contact them, after learning that there was a settlement of them only a few miles from the new northern rail terminal named Susuka (or Shishika).

The Ainu people, more numerous than the Oroki, also had many traditional remedies, usually decoctions of plants, or else animal substances. Bear's gall bladder was believed to be especially effective. It was first dried on a line over the fire in the center of the room, then a piece would be broken off for the patient to chew, or else it was powdered and mixed with water. A less obnoxious remedy was to tie around a child's neck a bag containing bits of milkweed, and ashes taken from the fireplace and thus sacred to the fire god.

The Ainu also claimed to have a form of exorcism to cure paralysis, the correct place for this being on the bank of a river. After being tied with strands of bulrushes around arms, body and legs, the patient was stroked with pebbles which were then put in a small wooden box. The exorcist would next pray in a singsong voice, stamping the right foot and stretching his or her arms skywards. Then the bulrushes were cut off the patient's body with a sickle, and used to beat the person lightly to the accompaniment of a hissing sound. Finally the box of stones was pushed into the river, with the sickle and bulrushes, to float away.

Appendix 4

The Jodo Shin School of Buddhism

Buddhism was introduced to Japan from Korea and China in the sixth century AD. For long its influence was limited to the court and nobility, its abstruse philosophy and esoteric practices having little to offer the hard-working peasant. The priests enjoyed imperial favor and riches, and were often more interested in politics than the religious life. Thus a great need for reform arose.

In the ninth century an Emperor sent two scholars to China to learn all they could of up-to-date teaching, to try to revitalize the religion. One of these men, Saicho, brought back all the Sutras he could find. These are sermons and dialogues by famous priests, later recognized as authentic teaching, somewhat similar to the position of Jewish Talmudic writings. Included in these were the various sectarian teachings of Chinese priests, many of them actually contradictory.

Thus the way of attaining Enlightenment was now left largely to individual choice. There was the original philosophical teaching, with its varied accretions of ascetic practices, esoteric mysteries, abstract contemplation, and removal of illusion; or a new possibility was now presented of salvation through the saving grace of a certain Amida, together with the practice of some of the usual former Buddhist rituals.

Some have claimed that this new idea was introduced to Buddhism in India before the time of Christ, but Taisei Michihata, a man born into a priestly family and himself a priest for over 20 years, states that this idea resulted from Christian influence. In his book *From Buddha to Christ* he says that as a priest he had access to locked storerooms of ancient manuscripts in certain temples, and there learned that the idea of an invocation to a higher power was of Christian origin. In its beginning Buddhism had no doctrine of a creator, and didn't recognize the existence of any gods, nor of the human soul. But by the tenth century a Sutra had appeared teaching the doctrine of a self-existent Buddha-creator. Michihata tells us Christianity gained so many con-

verts when it spread to India that the followers of Sakya Muni 'were com-
pelled to borrow that doctrine from their rivals, and set it forth in order to be
able to hold their own against the Christians'.

While in Japan little attention was paid, at first, to this new Sutra Saicho
had brought back, after some years the many contradictions existing in
Buddhist teaching brought mounting frustration to those who seriously sought
for meaning in their religious life. In 1117, a famous priest named Ryonin had
a vision of Amida, and travelled throughout Japan preaching about the grace
of Amida, although he also retained many of the old doctrines and practices.

Another priest, Honen, depressed after 20 years of fruitless effort to
attain Enlightenment, felt there must be some more practical and effective
way of universal salvation. In 1175 he found the following passage in a Sutra.
'Whether walking or standing, sitting or lying, only repeat the name of Amida
with all your heart. Never cease the practice of it even for a moment. This is
the very work which unfailingly issues in salvation, for it is in accord with the
original vow of that Buddha.'

He forthwith formed a new school of Buddhism called the Jodo (Pure
Land) Sect, and taught that just repeating the phrase 'Adoration to the Lord of
boundless light' as one's main religious duty, would, if accompanied by faith,
give assurance of rebirth in the Pure Land. He, too, however, continued some
of the old religious practices, and retained images of other Buddhas on the
altar.

Another man, Shinran, who had been ordained a priest at eight years of
age, heard Honen preach when he was 27, and realized this was what he was
seeking — a way of salvation for ordinary men. Both Honen and he were later
banished from Kyoto by the Emperor, at the insistence of jealous priests from
the old schools, and Shinran spent 28 years doing missionary work throughout
Japan.

It was he who formed the Jodo Shin (True Pure Land) Sect, to which the
Tamuras belonged. This elaborated on Honen's ideas, teaching that belief in
the invocation to Amida is sufficient to ensure salvation, and that that alone
has enough merit for rebirth in the Pure Land. Any further repetition of the
invocation is just prompted by gratitude for salvation, while the power to
exercise the necessary faith is also Amida's gift, and is not natural to man.
Good deeds were therefore irrelevant, since salvation is assured as soon as
there is faith.

This 'easy way' of Amidaism appealed strongly to the common people,
especially with its promise of life after death, and it soon had the largest
following of all Japanese schools of Buddhism. It had no ethical content,
however, having nothing to say about present life. Two centuries later, a
priest named Rennyo sought to remedy this weakness by adding that a saved
man should practise all the ordinary moralities, be faithful in his duty to the
state, and as a member of society and the home. But he rejected all other
religious practices.

In view of all this, it is not surprising that when many Japanese first hear the Christian Gospel they say, 'It's just like our Buddhism'. But neither they, nor most Christian workers, are usually aware of how this came about, or that it is completely contrary to original Buddhism with its aim of getting rid of all personal desire and losing individual consciousness in Nirvana. Saicho, however, is known to have had contact with Nestorian Christians in China, and Michihata said that in Kyoto there is a portion of the Bible copied by Shinran.

Appendix 5

*A Christian Funeral**

'The formal part of the ceremony was soon ended, and the lid of the coffin removed so that relatives and friends might bid him a last farewell. I moved forward with the others, and uttered a silent prayer. As I opened my eyes and saw the face of the man, a sudden wave of emotion passed over me. It did not look like the face of one who has passed through the gates of death. He looked like one.... in peaceful sleep.... not a trace of suffering visible anywhere; he seemed to be smiling! As I stood and gazed at him, I could read in his countenance the joy and peace with which his life had been filled.

'While in the temple service, I had conducted funerals without number..... the principal officiant in the mass which is supposed to conduct the soul of the deceased into Paradise.... In the end I came to loathe these services so deeply the very mention of a funeral made me shudder.

'The time taken by the whole thing (sutra reading, prayers, tonsure) is only about ten minutes, but during that time the priest must look almost continuously at the face of the corpse. Usually the head has been shaved roughly, the body has been wrapped in a single ragged garment (western Japan in the '20s), the knees are drawn up under the chin and the face has an expression like that of a person in a sleep filled with fear..... It is a sight one does not care to look upon a second time.

'When I looked at the face of Mr Watanabe that day, however, it was entirely different from anything I had ever seen before..... and stirred my soul to its very depths. The very glory of God seemed to shine out of that casket!'

*Description of the first Christian funeral he had attended, by ex-Buddhist priest Taisei Michihata. The funeral was that of a friend named Watanabe.